Creedal Apologetics

Creedal Apologetics

Learning to Use the Apostles' Creed to Defend
and Proclaim the Christian Faith

Nancy A. Almodovar

FOREWORD BY
Eric Rachut

RESOURCE *Publications* · Eugene, Oregon

CREEDAL APOLOGETICS
Learning to Use the Apostles' Creed to Defend and Proclaim the Christian Faith

Copyright © 2021 Nancy A. Almodovar. All rights reserved. Except for brief quotations in critical publications or reviews, no part of this book may be reproduced in any manner without prior written permission from the publisher. Write: Permissions, Wipf and Stock Publishers, 199 W. 8th Ave., Suite 3, Eugene, OR 97401.

Resource Publications
An Imprint of Wipf and Stock Publishers
199 W. 8th Ave., Suite 3
Eugene, OR 97401

www.wipfandstock.com

PAPERBACK ISBN: 978-1-7252-9759-3
HARDCOVER ISBN: 978-1-7252-9757-9
EBOOK ISBN: 978-1-7252-9758-6

03/15/21

Scripture quotations are from the ESV® Bible (The Holy Bible, English Standard Version®), copyright © 2001 by Crossway, a publishing ministry of Good News Publishers. Used by permission. All rights reserved.

In Gratitude

First, I want to thank God, my Father; Jesus Christ, my Lord and Savior who died, was buried and rose again for the forgiveness of my sins; and the Holy Spirit who uses his word and sacraments to create saving faith and through them strengthens my faith continually.

Second, to Dr. John Warwick Montgomery whose teaching through Trinity College and Seminary brought me into the field of apologetics. Without you introducing me to the defense of the faith, I would not be where I am. Thank you for your counsel and direction for my vocation.

Third, my pastor, Rev. Craig Kellerman, for his patience with me as I learned anew the beauty and treasure we have in God's word and sacraments and for your encouragement, faithful teaching of the Bible and friendship. Your love and kindness does not go unnoticed and I hope to be able to emulate that with those whom God allows me to proclaim or defend the gospel.

Fourth, the Ladies of Dorcas and those in the Tuesday Women's Bible Study, you are the best! You've become family to me and I love you so much for being there for me as I became Lutheran. Thank you for your support and love and especially enduring my many questions as I worked through bad theology into that which is good (Lutheran). Thank you also for sending me to the International Academy for Apologetics, Evangelism and Human Rights in Strasburg and for being the ones God used to fan the failing ember of evangelism back to a roaring fire. Thank you to Barb for working on the manuscript edits in a quick manner as the deadline crept up on us pretty swiftly this time.

To the men and women who attend the #ApologeticsTogether courses on my YouTube channel (Lutheran Girl). What began as lessons to help you in proclaiming and defending the faith, has developed into this book which you now hold. It is my hope that you have gained tools in your "evangelism toolbox" that you can grab when offering an apologetic to those you come into contact. It is my hope that you are now better equipped to give a reason for the hope we have within. May God give the increase!

To my husband, Bobby, you are simply amazing. You don't complain when I lock myself in my office to finish off a manuscript, article, or blog post. You continually encourage me to do this vocation (among many) which God has given me while managing to keep me sane as deadlines loom on the horizon. You are my best friend and greatest love of my life. I thank God continually for you.

Finally, to the reader: Thank you for picking up this book. It tells me that you want to proclaim the faith to the unbelievers around you and defend Christ to the skeptic. I only ask that you prayerfully engage in apologetics with the Creed as your guide and the Holy Scripture as the word proclaimed. You may plant or water but always remember, it is God who gives the increase. Rely on him and use this as a roadmap for your conversations. May the Lord bring many into his church and strengthen believers while they defend and proclaim his glorious gospel of the forgiveness of all our sins.

I believe in God, the Father Almighty,
Maker of heaven and earth.
And in Jesus Christ, His only Son, our Lord,
who was conceived by the Holy Spirit, born of the Virgin Mary,
suffered under Pontius Pilate, was crucified, died and was buried.
He descended into hell. The third day He rose again from
the dead. He ascended into heaven and sits at the right hand
of God the Father Almighty. From thence He will come to
judge the living and the dead.
I believe in the Holy Spirit,
the holy Christian Church,
the communion of saints,
the forgiveness of sins, the
resurrection of the body,
and the life everlasting. Amen.

Contents

Foreword by Eric Rachut | xi
Preface | xiii
Introduction: What Is Apologetics and Why Do We Do It? | xv

Chapter 1: Why a "Creedal Apologetic"? | 1
Chapter 2: First Things First | 14
Chapter 3: Creeds in the Bible? | 27
Chapter 4: Ancient Creeds | 48
Chapter 5: I Believe in God the Father | 69
Chapter 6: And in Jesus Christ | 82
Chapter 7: Born to Die | 91
Chapter 8: For You | 95
Chapter 9: Why the Resurrection Matters | 102
Chapter 10: The "What Now?" | 118
Chapter 11: Defending and Proclaiming the Faith | 127
Chapter 12: Carpe Diem | 137

Appendix | 145
Bibliography | 149

Foreword

> Always be prepared to make a defense [Greek *apologia*] to anyone who calls you to account for the hope that is in you, yet do it with gentleness and reverence. —1 Pet 3:15

APOLOGETICS, MEANING DEFENSE (AND evangelization) of the Christian faith by means of evidence, has fallen on hard times in America. Our secular society is often impatient with such objective presentations and prefers personal testimony, based on our own experiences. Dr. Almodovar, with a Pentecostal background and a theological education in confessional Lutheranism, well understands both of these approaches. In this book, she tells us why the apologetic method is the scriptural and, indeed, the more effective way. She goes further and explains how creeds, distillations of Christian truths, are embedded throughout Scripture itself and how they have emerged seamlessly into creeds of today. The earliest and most succinct, the Apostles' Creed, is easily recalled during our conversations with unbelieving friends, relatives, coworkers, and chance acquaintances, and can guide us both in what to say and also what not to say, culminating in the five golden words which are the heart and soul of Christianity.

Her students, including myself, thank her from our hearts for this vital book.

—Eric Rachut, MD

Preface

RECENTLY I BEGAN TEACHING an online course on apologetics via YouTube and Zoom (an online live video streaming service) in which I worked through the eyewitness accounts of the evangelists as the basis for engaging unbelievers and skeptics with the gospel of Jesus Christ. From the beginning I remarked that one of the first creeds given Christians is to be found in 1 Corinthians 15:3–4:

> For I delivered to you as of first importance what I also received: that Christ died for our sins in accordance with the Scriptures, that he was buried, that he was raised on the third day in accordance with the Scriptures, and that he appeared to Cephas then to the twelve. Then he appeared to more than five hundred brothers at one time, most of whom are still alive, though some have fallen asleep.

The gospel is the message Christians are to bring to a world dying apart from Jesus Christ. The gospel is what must dominate our conversations both within and without the church. What we believe must be informed by the Scriptures which point to Jesus Christ as the central message of the Christian faith. Yet, for many, answering the questions of unbelievers is one of the most frightful and challenging tasks to accomplish. Too many will forward the enquirer to their pastor instead of being able to give an apologetic (Greek *apologia*) or answer for their faith. How then are Christians to be able to defend and proclaim the faith? This is the question to be asked and answered for believers of every age.

> The early creeds themselves, and specifically Nicaea, were essentially apologetical. They were designed to clarify truth claims, and refute false claims. They were defenses of the core truths found

in the Scriptures themselves, without being exhaustive about the truth that is found in Scripture. So, to know these claims and defend them seems to be a task that still applies to us today as inheritors of an apostolic and historical Christian faith.[1]

Many modern evangelicals are unfamiliar with creeds, their history, importance and apologetic value when both learning about the faith and defending/proclaiming it with an unbeliever. The following questions will be dealt with in this book:

What is a creed?

Why creeds at all?

When were creeds first used?

Where do we find creeds?

How are creeds to be used?

Within the chapters of this book you will find answers to each of these questions and why using the Apostles' Creed will help you in answering questions about the Christian faith from the unbeliever. It is by using this creed that you will remember to stay on the essentials of the faith and not wander down some conversational or theological rabbit hole.

Throughout this book, you will come to learn that the New Testament's own apostle Paul utilized a creed, along with other creeds in his letters or from the other apostles and evangelists, given to him as he writes, "what I also received" (cf. 1 Cor 15). Since this is a Biblical practice we too may use these. Couple the biblical creeds with the Apostles' Creed, which as you will see is grounded in the Scriptures, and you gain a useful tool to aid in the removal of the skeptic's obstacles to faith while at the same time proclaim the beautiful gospel of grace. This is the reason behind this book and the purpose for which it is offered to you, the reader: Equipping you to defend and proclaim the Christian faith through the use of the early church creeds, specifically the Apostles' Creed.

Scripture quotes are from the English Standard Version unless specifically noted.

---

1. Costello, "Early Christian Creeds and Their Importance," para. 8.

INTRODUCTION

What Is Apologetics and Why Do We Do It?

What Is Apologetics?

IF WE ARE GOING to learn about apologetics utilizing the Creed (Apostles' Creed) then we should first begin with defining what is meant throughout this book by the term "apologetics." The base Greek root word means "defense" and in this context it is the defense of the Christian faith. Apologetics is not giving an excuse for our faith as in "I'm sorry for being a Christian" but it is a species of evangelism. It is the intellectual side of evangelism and is distinguished from that which comes from the heart. Apologetics deals with the intellectual difficulties that people may have in coming to conversion. Apologetics seeks to remove the hindrances to true faith that unbelievers and skeptics will place down as excuses not to believe. It pursues answers to questions while also remaining true to the gospel in its presentation. Apologetics utilizing the Creed as the guide to discussions will enable one to focus on the essentials rather than on one's own personal experience or various philosophical arguments. A Creedal apologetics then becomes a useful tool in the work of evangelism for believers of all ages.

The point or goal of apologetics is to move people along the road cluttered with their reasons not to believe the gospel, over the hurdles, removing stumbling blocks to get them to the Door (that's Jesus) at the house of salvation. It is not about answering every single question. It is not about arguing but defending. It is not about debates but discussing and proclaiming Jesus who died, was buried, and rose again according to the Scriptures. As Christians we rely upon the Holy Spirit who works through the means of grace to grant saving faith and one of those means is the proclaimed word of God, the Bible. As Christians we must then rely upon the Holy Spirit to guide our

INTRODUCTION: WHAT IS APOLOGETICS AND WHY DO WE DO IT?

conversation and enable us to proclaim the gospel of Jesus Christ which is the "power of God unto salvation" (Rom 1:17).

God, working through the means of grace (word and sacraments of holy baptism and the Lord's Supper) grants true faith and the forgiveness of sins. Primarily, when working with an unbeliever, God will use the proclaimed word, either in formal (church) or informal (one-on-one) situations. It does not matter where the word is proclaimed, only that it is proclaimed. Scripture informs us that the gospel itself is "the power of God for salvation to everyone who believes " (Rom 1:16 ESV) It is not our elegance or eloquence that wins the day but God, by his Holy Spirit, moves through the word and brings about faith in his dear Son, our Lord Jesus Christ, in the heart of the unbeliever. Defending the faith, using the Apostles' Creed, enables the believer to proclaim Christ crucified and risen again and remain on the essentials of the Christian faith.

Questions and Answers

People have questions. Christians should have the answers. As I will repeat throughout various parts of this book, apologetics is not about debate and certainly not about winning the argument. It is about answering the questions that unbelievers have regarding the Christian faith. In my little neighborhood there is a large populace which has never been to church. They only know about Christianity from what they hear on television. Sadly, much of that is not true Christianity. As a believer living next door to them, it is my duty, in my love for God, to love my neighbor. In loving them it is crucial that I am praying for them and asking God to pique their interest in Christianity. Many of my own neighbors know that my husband and I attend church on Sunday and even various Bible studies throughout the week. Often, they will come and ask us questions. This is the duty of every believer: to answer questions...as best you can.

Now, you may not have all the answers. In fact, none of us do. However, the word of God does have those answers and we should be so well-versed in them that the Holy Spirit can draw upon the Scriptures and answer them. Through knowing and understanding the Apostles' Creed, you maintain a useful outline of the essentials of the Christian faith from which to guide the discussions to the most important matter, that of eternal life or death. These statements in the Apostles' Creed answers the questions regarding God, Jesus, the Holy Spirit, and the forgiveness of sins.

INTRODUCTION: WHAT IS APOLOGETICS AND WHY DO WE DO IT?

Their many questions may involve: Who is God? Who is the Creator? Why do you believe in Jesus? How do you know he really existed? Who is the Holy Spirit? What happens when I die? What happens if the world ends? A question that matters to their eternity is what the Apostles' Creed reminds us is truly the difference between life and death. The Creed enables you to keep the conversation zeroing in on God and his "greatest treasure for us,"[1] his dear Son Jesus Christ and his death, burial, and resurrection according to the Scriptures. These are, after all, the most important questions to answer.

Why Do We Do Apologetics?

The thrust of apologetics is to move people through their obstructions to the reasons for Christianity and into the "house of salvation." As Dr. John Warwick Montgomery has taught, if we view the question part of the discussion with unbelievers as a path where the end is the "house of salvation," then apologetics is the removing of stones and stumbling blocks along that way.[2] We are to move the individual unbeliever to the offense of the cross where the person has to face a choice between attempting to save himself or believe that Jesus died for them and paid for their sins so that they may have eternal life. It is the thrust of apologetics to get people to recognize the crossroad that is the sacrificial death of Jesus on the cross and that their choice as to whether they insist on saving themselves or embracing that Christ died for them. It moves past all the other arguments and brings us to this fork in the road, namely Jesus Christ. At the end of the path of questions, we Christians, having removed all reasons to not believe, leave the unbeliever at the Door of salvation at the house of salvation. Either by the grace of God they come to faith in Jesus for the forgiveness of sins or they turn away to their own destruction.

Christians, utilizing the legitimate defense of the faith against objections, work through those arguments bringing the validity of Christianity and its claims to the individual. Creedal apologetics, helping us to remain focused on the essentials, is then a tool that is in our toolbox of evangelism equipment as an aide to filling in gaps and holes where other tools such as personal testimony cannot fill in or bridge the gap. No believer's spiritual toolbox

---

1. Dau, *Concordia*, 399.
2. He said this at the International Academy for Apologetics, Evangelism and Human Rights in Strasbourg France in 2019.

should be without this fine, well-tested tool and they should be skilled in using it. Not everyone is going to come to faith in Christ because of a heartfelt testimony, due to its subjectivity. Some individuals want objective truth. By utilizing the Apostles' Creed, the Christian will answer for the faith they have while being reminded to remain on the essentials of the faith.

What About the Work of the Holy Spirit in Apologetics?

The Holy Spirit holds the primary place within apologetics. The arguments and evidences of the faith are not the basis alone upon which people enter the "house of salvation." Crucial to the new birth is the grace of God moving upon the spiritually dead person, quickening them and granting them the gift of faith. However, unlike pietism, we do not believe that God mysteriously moves upon the person without also dealing with them on an intellectual level. God uses means by which to work. Through the hearing of the gospel God may grant true faith.

These means of grace, the ways God has ordained to bring saving faith to sinners, are the ways the Holy Spirit works. While Lutherans and Calvinists are comfortable with the term "the means of grace," evangelicals operate similarly without calling it by that name. Evangelicals will agree that through preaching and teaching of the Word, God convicts and converts sinners to Christ. That is a means of grace. As a Christian defending the faith you will use the word of God and God has told us that it is through hearing that faith comes (cf. Rom 10: 17). God has told us that God uses the foolishness of preaching to bring life. God has told us that the Gospel is the power of God unto salvation (Rom 1:17). God has said that through the hearing of faith we receive the Holy Spirit (Gal 3:2). (I speak of adult conversions here where they believe and then are baptized for the forgiveness of their sins.)

Furthermore, Jesus said that eternal life was to "know God" (cf. John 17:3) and that is speaking to the intellect, not just the heart. Apologetics is the presentation of the gospel in a systematic and organized way which deals with the specific questions of the unbeliever steering them and directing them ever closer to the cross and the offense of the cross. What a great and useful tool we have been given in the Apostles' Creed which is broken into three parts (Father, Son and Holy Spirit) and by its own breakdown enables us to stay on the essentials. Through the use of the Creed in apologetics, in answering their questions, you bring to them the whole gospel. As

I've written repeatedly, Paul tells us in Romans 1:16 that the gospel is the power of God unto salvation and in Corinthians that it is through the foolish preaching of the cross that people are saved. The crux of the gospel is within the Apostles' Creed and, therefore, Christians would only benefit from reading and studying it—the verses for each section, the reasoning behind it, the history—and learning how the early church used it, not only for adult new believers, but also as a reason for the faith within.

The Apostles' Creed (hereafter, the Creed) reminds us of the essentials of the faith. Therefore, even if we gave an insurmountable pile of evidence to the veracity of Jesus, his life, his death, the miracles he performed, the resurrection, which indeed we have, it would be of no effect without the Holy Spirit. The gospel must be proclaimed and the Creed equips you to proclaim it to the world.

The Holy Spirit uses that evidence, making the Scriptures true to the hearer, opening their ears to hear and to understand, to bring the person to the cross and to recognize their need of a Savior. Though we have such an arsenal, if we were to rely upon our skills of argumentation, our powers of evidence, our three-point sermons on the validity of the resurrection, it would never be enough to convince a person of the truth of the gospel without the Holy Spirit moving upon the heart and mind of the individual and giving them new life. We are never to rely solely upon apologetics alone to convince a person of their need of the cross for it is the work of the Holy Spirit to convict them of their sins and unrighteousness and to work on the very will of the person to come to Christ.

What Apologetics Is Not

Very often, Christians have this view of apologetics as arguing, winning the debate, presenting your denomination, defending your view of the end times and/or just getting them to believe in "a god." This is not what apologetics is about. Rather, it is answering for the faith and hope that you have in Jesus Christ. As Saint Peter writes, "but in your hearts honor Christ the Lord as holy, always being prepared to make a defense to anyone who asks you for a reason for the hope that is in you" (1 Pet 3:16). It is a tool within the evangelism toolbox that you will need to pull out at some point when proclaiming the gospel to an unbeliever.

Rather than winning the argument, or just plain arguing a point, biblical apologetics is about presenting reasons to believe. It is not about "soul winning." That's God's business. It is not even about winning the argument, but about presenting the reasons for the Christian faith. Our focus in apologetics is to be the gospel of Jesus Christ through the presentation of the eyewitness accounts via the evangelists and the New Testament document.

Instead of defending your view of the Last Days it is about defending the death, burial, and resurrection of Jesus Christ as an historic event with eyewitnesses. No one knows enough about eschatology (end times) to defend it and too much of today's ideas are based on the errant movements of Restorationism in the seventeenth and eighteenth centuries. Instead of getting the skeptic to agree that there is a god, a great designer, or master builder of this universe, it is introducing them to Jesus Christ as the only way to the Father (John 14:6), Maker of Heaven and Earth.

The gospel, and use of apologetics in the proclamation of the forgiveness of sins, is also *not* about your testimony. We are to proclaim Christ and him being crucified, buried, and raised from the dead according to the scriptures. Personal testimony is too subjective and open to speculation, questions and doubt, even by the person subjectively experiencing this. It is best to stay on the objective truths of salvation and with a creedal apologetic you will not fall into the mud and muck of subjective testimony.

What Is the Goal of Apologetics?

If apologetics isn't about me sharing what happened to me (although that may be a starting point), what is it about? Why should we engage in defending the faith and answering their questions? Sadly, a London Baptist preacher once denounced defending the faith saying that a lion doesn't need any defense it just needs to be released from the cage it's in. Scripture would not tell us to have a defense ready if we weren't supposed to be prepared. We become lazy Christians when we do not prepare to defend the faith, study to show ourselves approved workmen or have a reason for the hope that is in us. We must do the work necessary to be able to answer their questions.

As to personal testimony, let's face it, the gospel does affect us personally and individually and so we do have a testimony. However, the gospel is only about you as far as sin is concerned, that you too needed to be washed from your sins and justified before a Holy God. However, I encourage you to get off the subjective as quickly as you can and plant your feet firmly in creedal apologetics which is all about objective truth. You'll be much safer there and can answer their questions with verifiable facts instead of your personal feelings. After all, apologetics is about proclaiming the life, death, and resurrection of Jesus for the forgiveness of the sins of the world. The goal is to bring the person to the "house of salvation," a term used by my first apologetics professor, Dr. John Warwick Montgomery. He taught us that we are to bring them past all the hurdles the unbeliever will put up, down the narrow path, to the Door of salvation. It is then up to the Holy Spirit to bring them into the house, the Christian faith.

The task of the apologist is to move people along the road to the Door of salvation through answering their questions and removing stumbling blocks. At times, you may have a discussion about a particular reason they say they have to remain in their unbelief, so you might need to remain on that topic for a while. However, once you remove that stumbling block, there will be another and another until they are all removed and the skeptic must come to one of two conclusions:

These are true and then repent believing on Jesus for the forgiveness of their sins.

OR

This is not true, thereby remaining in their sins.

I mention bringing them to the Door of salvation at the house of salvation. The proper way of understanding the "house of salvation" is to understand that it is the ultimate point at which the unbeliever comes to deal with their questions with regard to the Christian faith. We have brought them along the road of evidentiary proof, have shared the law and the gospel with them along with those proofs, and now they stand at the Door of salvation, which is Christ. It is here that they read the sign, "Believe," and the most pivotal moment is upon them.

The goal of apologetics is to bring the good news of Jesus' life, death, burial, and resurrection to the world. If by the use of the Creed we believers are better equipped, then it is a tool we should know how to use in answering the questions of skeptics and unbelievers.

Apologetics Done Right!

Apologetics, when done properly, should bring people to the offense of the cross. It should bring them to the understanding that the message of the gospel is true and that there is a Savior to trust and believe in. Preaching tells the glorious message bringing home the fact that we have all broken the laws of God and God himself has propitiated for us and there is grace available to us by the cross of Christ. Together apologetics and preaching work to ultimately bring the unbeliever to the crossroad (no pun intended) of their life where they will either embrace Christ as Lord and Savior or they will reject him hoping somehow to save themselves. In its simplest form, preaching is the message of the law and gospel while apologetics is the presenting of the many evidences for the validity of that message.

Recently I read a blog where the apologist was complaining that after a debate they were participating in, the organizers had a few people come up and testify to the validity of the faith and its life-changing force. This was "testimony time" and used emotions and subjective experiences to validate Biblical truths. The skeptics rightly called it a "bait and switch" tactic. This is not how to proclaim the gospel. Therefore, we need to think of apologetics as a tool in our evangelism toolbox. It is one way to bring to the forefront the faith, defending the faith as well as proclaiming the faith using the objective testimonies, eyewitness accounts, and documentary proofs of the Scripture. What better way than to utilize the Apostles' Creed, as was done in the ancient church and for centuries? If you remain on your own experiences, then you are not presenting the faith, proclaiming the gospel properly but rather your opinion. Unless you are presenting the Christ through whom all the worlds were made, then you are not doing the actual task of apologetics and, therefore, not presenting the life-giving Gospel. Instead, you're just defending a view or your own subjective experiences. Real apologetics is evangelistic because the purpose is to bring them to the house of salvation, to Christ Jesus who died for the forgiveness of their sins.

What is needed is a Spirit-controlled apologetic that aggressively challenges the subjective approach structure of modern evangelicalism and insists that a proper proclamation be based upon the patterns exemplified by the apostles and earliest Christians as evidenced by their sermons in the book of Acts, and codified and exemplified in Creedal Apologetics. Men and women today must be brought to the realization that emotions and subjective experiences do not validate truth and that the Christian faith is based upon objective, eyewitness testimony and documentary evidence.

The apostles themselves, who touched, lived with, and ate with Jesus, saw his crucifixion, and witnessed the transfiguration of our Lord (Matt 17:1–9), moved from those experiences to Biblical verification. Matthew reminds us that Jesus has provided forgiveness of sins conquering death and the grave "as the scriptures foretold," therefore, how much more must we believers, who have not personally seen these things, move off of our subjective experiences or personal testimonies back onto the fulfilled word of God?

The apostle Peter, writing about the experience on the Mount of Transfiguration, later wrote:

> We were eyewitnesses of his [Jesus'] majesty... we ourselves heard this very voice borne from heaven, for we were with him on the holy mountain. And we have something more sure, the prophetic word, to which you will do well to pay attention as to a lamp shining in a dark places. (2 Pet 1:16–20)

Everything the apostles experienced pales in comparison to the "more sure word" of God. Peter relied upon the Scriptures more than his own experiences. Therefore, we are wise to move away from our own experiences and proclaim the testimony of the prophets and apostles since their word is "more sure."

The answer to this dilemma is simple: Keep to the essentials via a Creedal apologetic. Believers must move quickly from testifying of their own personal experience, away from their own denominational peculiarities and subjective experiences, on to the gospel of Christ and him being crucified and rising again. The reason for defending the faith is to bring the unbeliever to the foot of the cross so that, by the grace of God, they might repent and believe in him. Believers of all theological backgrounds must focus back on the gospel. Utilizing a Creedal apologetic will help us stay on point and on the word, just like the apostles.

Our task as believers is not to know every possible hurdle the unbeliever puts in front of us. However, it is to gently lead them down that road and bring that message of true hope home. If they have questions you do not have the answer to, be honest and tell them you will get back to them. However, when they walk away, whether or not they have come to true faith, they should understand you have presented to them the Way, the Truth, and the Life. By utilizing the Apostles' Creed you are able to stay on point, quickly remember the essentials of the faith, and present to them Jesus who died, was buried, and rose again on the third day according to the Scriptures, for the forgiveness of all of our sins (1 Cor 15).

INTRODUCTION: WHAT IS APOLOGETICS AND WHY DO WE DO IT?

The Apostles' Creed and Scripture

I grew up in a Holiness Pentecostal church which did not place any value on the creeds nor on much of church history (except what happened after the Restoration movement in the mid-1800s). Therefore, I did not know that you can find the phrases from the Apostles' Creed in the Scriptures. No theologian worth their salt is going to say the apostles wrote this creed. However, any Christian who knows church history knows that it is based upon the word of God. So, in this brief segment I'm going to reference the verses with the various phrases of the Apostles' Creed:

I believe in God, the Father Almighty (Matt 5:45)

Creator of heaven and earth (Gen 1–2; Rom 1:20)

And in Jesus Christ, His only Son, our Lord (Matt 3:17; Phil 2:12)

Who was conceived by the Holy Spirit (Luke 1:35)

Born of the Virgin Mary (Luke 2:7)

Suffered under Pontius Pilate (John 19:16)

Was crucified, died, and was buried. (John 19:29–42)

He descended into hell (1 Pet 3:19–20)

On the third day He rose again from the dead (Matt 28:1–10; John 20:11–18)

He ascended into heaven (Luke 24:51)

And sits at the right hand of God (Heb 1:3)

The Father Almighty (Mark 14:36)

From thence He shall come again (Matt 16:27; Acts 10:39)

To judge the living and the dead (1 Cor 15:51)

I believe in the Holy Spirit (John 14:15–20; Acts 1:7–8)

The Holy Catholic Church (Matt 16:18–19; Eph 5:26–27; Col 1:24)

The forgiveness of sins (John 20:22–23)

The resurrection of the body (1 Cor 15:51–54; 1 Thess 4:13–18)

And the life everlasting (1 John 5:20)

While there are many more verses from God's word that would show these phrases are scriptural, I included these so that my Christian friends who feel uneasy about using it as a guide in their apologetic endeavors will see these are faithful statements of what the church universal has confessed for two millennia.

CHAPTER 1

Why a "Creedal Apologetic"?

DR. JOHN WARWICK MONTGOMERY, at his International Academy of Apologetics, Evangelism & Human Rights,[1] in Strasbourg, France, has insisted that when answering for the faith we present a creedal apologetic. The reasoning is that the creeds in the New Testament and the Apostles' Creed (along with the Nicene and Athanasian Creeds) offer the believer a way to remember the important teachings and doctrines of the Christian church. Those who have memorized the Apostles' Creed since childhood may more easily recall these "I believe . . ." statements to mind when engaging with the unbeliever. However, it is offered to all Christians, for all times, to use both as a reminder of what the church confesses and a guide to help you stay on those essentials when engaged with unbelievers and skeptics of the faith.

Today's Christians need to commit them to memory too so that they may more easily draw upon them in conversations regarding what we believe and why we believe it. This enables the believer to recall the key points of Christianity without getting bogged down in nonessentials. It equips the believer with what must be believed in order to be a Christian and helps to share those truths with the non-Christian and not get onto such subjective matters as testimony or opinion. The Creed helps the Christian to stay on the essentials of the faith.

Martin Luther writes that the "faith" (what he called the Apostles' Creed) "is to be explained for the common people in a way that can stand alone."[2] He followed the early church pattern of using the Creed for two reasons: To instruct the new believer in the faith and answer the questions

1. See http://www.apologeticsacademy.eu/.
2. Peters, "Luther's Understanding of the Apostles' Creed," 4.

of unbelievers. By using the Creed, believers affirm that the Triune God has revealed himself as Creator of the world and Savior of those who place their trust in his Son Jesus Christ. As a tool of apologetics the unbeliever learns that while they may "yearn for a relationship with the one creator God, they remain under the holy God's judgment of wrath for as long a time as God's free grace in Jesus has not yet been opened to them through the Spirit."[3] Luther argued that this Creed is the "summation of the Gospel" and it is that very message which we are to give as an answer when asked why we believe. What better to use than that which actually says "I believe . . . "? This Creed gives us a way to proclaim the forgiveness of sins to those still under God's wrath.

The goal which every Christian should have, when engaged in apologetics, is to bring people beyond their obstacles and to the cross of Christ. That is the reason we proclaim and defend the faith. Apart from this focus on the gospel we are simply having conversations that are much ado about nothing. The point of proclamation and a defense of the faith is to bring them to the Door of salvation, having removed the obstacles they put up against belief. God has given us wonderful tools in his word and in the Ecumenical Creeds which express the essence of the faith passed down to us.

The very meaning of creed (Latin *credo*) is to believe. Over the last hundred-plus years many Pentecostals and evangelicals have rejected creeds and placed the ultimate value upon experience. A proper defense of the Gospel is proclaiming what is believed in the objective sense. There is not one person alive today who was there at the time of the life, death and resurrection of Jesus. Therefore, proving him to be the fulfillment of the promises of the Old Testament prophets is reliant upon the eyewitness testimony of the Evangelists which we find in the Gospels and Acts and not our feelings or personal experiences. Creedal statements of the Christian faith simplify the gospel and continue the pattern set by John, Mark, Peter, Paul, James, and others in making declarative statements of objective and verifiable truths. Evangelicalism tends to reject this type of proclamation for a subjective presentation of their experiences, inner light, and personal testimony. This results in opinion when we are to present the facts of the Christian faith.

The strength of Creedal statements is that they are based upon the objective truths of Scripture. They can be verified because they appeal to eyewitness testimony of the historic events of Jesus Christ. They do not dwell

---

3. Peters, "Luther's Understanding of the Apostles' Creed," 5.

on subjective experiences of the day, miracles et al., but emphasize their eyewitness testimony. This is the documented proof God has gifted to the church and can be verified as fact because the events occurred within the personal knowledge of the writers. The Evangelists are the eyewitnesses that matter. Your personal testimony doesn't save. However, God promises that his gospel is the very power of salvation for all (Rom 1:17).

The weakness of an experience-based proof is that too often they do not agree with each other. Also, our sinful hearts are poor and untrustworthy interpreters of our own experiences. As in the case of the issue of the Trinity within the early days of Pentecostalism, tongues and interpretation decided upon that doctrine. While one side insisted that God was indeed three persons in unity, a tongue and interpretation disagreed with that historic, biblical, and creedal statement. Therefore a modern Modalism arose, and many left the fellowship (Assemblies of God) and created the United Pentecostal Church. Subjective experience dictated doctrine and led many into heresy.[4]

An Apostolic Apologetic Pattern

The Bible has a very short and simplified view of what the Gospel is:

> For I delivered to you as of first importance what I also received: that Christ died for our sins in accordance with the Scriptures, ⁴ that he was buried, that he was raised on the third day in accordance with the Scriptures, ⁵ and that he appeared to Cephas, then to the twelve. ⁶ Then he appeared to more than five hundred brothers at one time, most of whom are still alive, though some have fallen asleep. ⁷ Then he appeared to James, then to all the apostles. (1 Cor 15:3–7)

Note well that Paul does not say the gospel is about your experiences, dreams, visions, tongues, and interpretation. The apostle does not say that it is about your experience. Instead he states what is of first importance:

1. Christ died for our sins.

2. Fulfilled prophecies—in the burial and resurrection of Jesus Christ "in accordance with the Scriptures."

---

4. Almodovar, *Modern Ninety-Five*, 8.

3. Objective truth—eyewitnesses are called upon by name: Cephas, James, the original disciples, and more than five hundred people.

The gospel proclamation given in the Scriptures for us to proclaim is not about our experience or testimony. In a recent article in the *Evangel* (Assemblies of God's primary publication), Fabien states that our personal testimony is crucial to proclamation. He writes, "Jesus interprets evangelism as our personal testimony."[5]

However, a biblical apologetic method based upon our own experience lacks the ability to prove the message of the life, death, and resurrection of Jesus Christ, thereby debilitating a proper gospel proclamation. Subjective proclamations from personal experience which cannot be validated leaves the gates wide open for the unbeliever to reject it based upon its subjective nature and their own personal experience. When utilizing a subjective experience, Christians have no right to require belief because every other world religion and cult follows the same pattern. This threadbare pattern of personal experience either via visions, dreams, or hearing from God gives no substance to take hold. It quickly unravels when confronted with various objections to the true Gospel. The skeptic may reasonably retort with their own spiritual experiences as validating their opinion. Thankfully, God has not left us to using our own subjective personal testimony. He has given us objective truth based upon historical facts and eyewitness testimony and must utilize these to remove any and all obstacles placed down as a reason for them to remain in their unbelief.

> Had the church always maintained its objective guide, this long disastrous period would never have occurred.[6]

Quite the bold statement made by Rev. Christensen, in his work regarding the subjective proclamation by modern evangelicals, and yet, it should be heeded carefully. Modern Evangelicalism has taken its eyes off of objective truth from the start and created a foundation in the marsh of subjective experience. Instead of continuing to proclaim the simple gospel which God had used for nearly two millennia to grow his church, they sought to focus on experiences and personal testimony. Many of us who come out of evangelical churches know this pattern well. However, the pattern we find in the Scriptures is objective based on the eyewitness testimony of the Apostles and early church.

5. Fabien, "Evangelism as a Testimony," para. 3.
6. Christensen, "Subjective and Objective Religion (Part 1)," para. 6.

WHY A "CREEDAL APOLOGETIC"?

If evangelism is about the Gospel then certainly apologetics is about giving answers for the faith we have in the message of the Gospel.

Refusing the Gift of "the Creed"

The historic creeds of the ancient church give us statements taken from the Scriptures but in the ultimate sense, they are "pregnant summaries"[7] of the Bible. They are "childlike faith statements"[8] and "the most compact formulation of the self-revelation of God the Father through his Son by means of the Holy Spirit."[9] They concisely articulate what is necessary to know about God and his salvation and the forgiveness of sins. These brief statements tell a dying world what they truly need to hear: God is their Creator, Jesus is their Savior, the Holy Spirit is their Sanctifier, and Jesus is returning to judge the living and the dead.

Therefore, rejecting the historical creeds of the church set modern evangelicals adrift on the sea of subjectivism. Loosing the moorings which attached modern evangelicals to the historic Christian church meant meandering on their own forays to validate their belief in Jesus Christ. Tossed to and fro by waves of feelings, subjective experiences, or opinions, they have often been wrecked on shallow shores, both damaging the gospel and risking the lives and assurances of those onboard. Anchoring the Christian to the ancient creeds is what the church today needs so desperately to avoid shipwrecking their own souls.

Today's Christian is no less indebted to the ancient church than Saint Paul was. When Saint Paul uses the term "delivered to you" in his letter to the Corinthians, he is delivering a creed, a statement of belief, which was passed down from the original apostles to him. Paul is giving the Corinthians a creedal statement about the gospel. To Paul there was nothing more important than the gospel which he "received" (1 Cor 15:3). The Lutheran Study Bible Notes remind us that

> These words [from 1 Cor 15] form the heart of the Apostles' Creed, which summarized the Gospel for the early Christians. What is

---

7. Peters, "Luther's Understanding of the Apostles' Creed," 5.
8. Peters, "Luther's Understanding of the Apostles' Creed," 5.
9. Peters, "Luther's Understanding of the Apostles' Creed," 5.

the Gospel? That Jesus died, was buried and rose again according to the Scriptures.

Just as Saint Paul and the Evangelists proclaimed the facts, the historical events of the life, death, burial, and resurrection of Jesus, so too must we. As Simon Greenleaf wrote, "The foundation of our religions is a basis of fact—the facts of the birth, ministry, miracles, death and resurrection of Jesus by the Evangelists as having actually occurred, within their own personal knowledge."[10] This is the foundation upon which believers are to stand and utilizing the ancient creeds equips us with biblical truths that are objectively provable.

Apostolic proclamation (the Kerygma)

1. Centered in God's redemptive work in Christ
2. Fulfillment of prophecy
3. Forgiveness of sins in the name of Jesus

Apostles' Creed

I believe in God, the Father Almighty, maker of heaven and earth.

And in Jesus Christ, His only Son, our Lord, who was conceived by the Holy Spirit, born of the Virgin Mary, suffered under Pontius Pilate, was crucified, died and was buried.

He descended into hell. The third day He rose again from the dead. He ascended into heaven and sits at the right hand of God the Father Almighty. From thence He will come to judge the living and the dead.

I believe in the Holy Spirit, the holy Christian Church, the communion of saints, the forgiveness of sins the resurrection of the body, and the life everlasting. Amen.

Note the simplicity of the second part (italics) of the Apostles' Creed in describing exactly what the Apostle Paul wrote in 1 Corinthians 15:

1 Corinthians 15:3–7—The Apostle Paul	The Apostles' Creed
Delivered to us	*I believe*
Christ	In *Jesus Christ*

10. Greenleaf, "Testimony of the Evangelists," para. 3.

WHY A "CREEDAL APOLOGETIC"?

1 Corinthians 15:3–7—The Apostle Paul	The Apostles' Creed
Died for our sins according to the Scriptures	Crucified, *died*
Buried	*Buried*
Raised on the *third day* according to the Scriptures	*Third day* He rose again from the dead

When the apostle Paul says "delivered to us" it is a creedal statement, a statement which says both we and the church universal believe and have passed on to each new believer this "I/We believe." Saint Paul wasn't saying anything new. It is believed that this creed was developed early in the Christian church, no later than two to three years after the resurrection.[11] This creed is nearly as old as Christianity itself and the apostle Paul is reminding the believers in Corinth of its truth and how all true Christians hold to this confession as fact.

In the same vein, the Apostles' Creed begins with "I believe." Moving from the Father to the Son and the Holy Spirit, Christians affirm that these are the truths "delivered to us" down the eons. These truths, though generations may question, though doubts may arise, though distortions may come, never truly go away. They may be overshadowed by error, expunged by heretics, and remain unlearned by everyday Christians, but these are the truths to hold and proclaim. For modern evangelicals creeds may seem too ordered and rigid. However, the creeds of the church are based upon a history of God's people putting the essential elements of the faith in a simple form to teach both new believers, build up the older saint, and/or answer the questions of skeptics alike.

As you see from the chart, the Apostles' Creed is quite similar to the Creed that Paul tells us of in 1 Corinthians. Modern Christians would benefit from having both this portion of Scripture (1 Cor. 15:3-7) and the Apostles' Creed memorized. That Paul appeals to eyewitnesses who are still alive when he penned his letter to the churches in Corinth only helps solidify the historicity of the events. Eyewitness testimony is crucial to prove cases presented in courts of law and written documents by those eyewitnesses are just as valid as their live testimony. Christians should never separate the proclamation and defense of the faith from its historic context nor from creedal statements made by the apostles and the early church.

---

11. Dau, *Concordia*, 398.

What About Personal Testimony?

There is no need to deny that each Christian has a testimony regarding their salvation, but anything beyond that needs to be verified against the one single standard of truth God has given to his people throughout all time: the written word of God. As will be shown in the final chapter, even the apostles, working miracles, healings and speaking in other tongues, never stopped at those subjective experiences but quickly moved on to the death and resurrection of Jesus Christ as authenticated by eyewitness testimony as the proclamation of grace and the apologetics that all Christians are to utilize with unbelievers and skeptics (cf. 2 Pet 1:16–21).

From the earliest days of the Restoration Movement (ca. 1830s onward) through Pentecostal, charismatic, and Third Wave, the focus has been upon subjective experiences of visions, dreams, and prophecies. It is these which are utilized in defending the faith with an infrequent nod to the multitude of evidence given in the Scriptures. Rather than appealing to the evangelists and their eyewitness testimony to the resurrection of Christ, today the personal testimony is emphasized both in local meetings and one on one. Evangelism as testimony[12] is seen as the way to convince an unbeliever of the truth of the gospel. Fabien argues, in his article, that since the apostles defended the faith by miracle and as eyewitnesses, today's Christians must also be eyewitnesses of God's miraculous power in order to be effective evangelists.[13] However, it has been shown that the proof should be grounded within the eyewitness testimonies of the apostles and prophets.

Modern Evangelicals, Pentecostals, charismatics, and others must quickly move from the subjective to the objective. By remaining upon their personal experiences they create a serious problem in both proclaiming and defending the faith. They relegate Christianity to the same level as other religions who also emphasize that their truth is based upon experience and not objective evidence. Removing the focus upon eyewitness testimony and documentary proofs leaves the Christian with nothing more to offer than the Mormon who emphasizes their "burning of the bosom" as proof of the Latter-day Saint teachings. Subjective experience proves nothing. Objective facts are what we've been given and that is what we must use.

---

12. Fabien, "Evangelism as a Testimony."
13. Fabien. *Evangelism*

Objective Defense

By using the Creed as a guideline for our discussions with unbelievers it should enable us to stay on the subject at hand. Our goal, in apologetics, is to remove reasons for unbelief and to proclaim the good news of the forgiveness of sins through Jesus Christ. Don't get sidetracked. Keeping the three parts of the Creed in the forefront of our minds helps us avoid the many rabbit trails that can form and moves us from the actual gospel message into areas of questions which are mere speculation rather than the objective truth of Jesus's life, death, burial, and resurrection.

That is the message we are to focus on: the resurrection. Saint Paul reminds us that apart from the resurrection of Jesus we are still in our sins and Christians should be pitied. However, the resurrection of Jesus, on the third day, is pivotal to everything else Jesus claimed to be. If he did not rise from the dead then everything he taught or did can rightfully be called into question. The gospel itself can be questioned because unless he rose from the dead, we are all still in our sins and lost eternally. Without the resurrection there is no gospel to proclaim or defend

As Christians we should know not only what we believe but why we believe it. Learn doctrine. In my YouTube class I reiterate time and again the importance of knowing basic Christian teachings. Luther reminds us that the Creed is a summary of the essential points of the gospel message. This book is going to get into each of the three parts of the Apostles Creed as Martin Luther divided them. It will then show you how each of the three sections, which are Father, Son and Holy Spirit, can help you to formulate an answer for your faith. When an evolutionist doubts there is a God, you can share "God the Father, Creator of heaven and earth." When a person, who may fret or think they are just not good enough to get to heaven, you would then share that Jesus died for the forgiveness of sins. Then, if one wonders what happens at the end of time you may assure them that believers will be raised from the dead and given life everlasting. Each section may be utilized because they each contain the most concise form of the doctrines of the Christian faith. To know the Apostles' Creed is the responsibility of every believer so that they can "give an answer for the faith within" (1 Peter 3:15).

CREEDAL APOLOGETICS

It's Not About You!

The gospel is not about you except that you too are a sinner in need of the forgiveness of sins. Time and again at the church I grew up in the focus of Friday or Sunday night service was testimony time. You would get up and share how you came to Christ and how bad a sinner you were before that. Too often the testimonies overemphasized the person's experiences and did not focus enough upon the forgiveness of sins or that Jesus, because he rose from the dead, had paid for all your sins so that you don't have to. You are not the point of the gospel message no matter how dramatic your conversion experience (I speak to those reading this book who were not baptized as infants and/or grew up in modern evangelistic churches). Your own experiences are too subjective to offer the unbeliever verifiable evidence. The gospel, however, is based upon objective truth written down for us by eyewitnesses. Therefore, you are never to be the focus of the conversation with the unbeliever except to say that you too are a great sinner in need of a great savior. The gospel is about the life, death, burial, and resurrection of Jesus Christ according to the Scriptures. So, make sure you move from your experiences to what Jesus did as objectively evidenced by the eyewitness testimony of the evangelists in the New Testament.

While too many modern Evangelicals believe that the church was crippled in the past by teaching the doctrines and creeds,[14] what they have really done is destroy the gospel proclamation having handicapped itself by refusing to use the tools given for a proper defense. Focusing upon subjective experience and other subjective things, which cannot be proven, has resulted in new converts not being equipped to stand against the torrent of attacks on the one true faith in Jesus Christ. Experiences do not continue forever and to base one's hopes upon a foundation of sand is to have the house of salvation fall when storms rise. Modern Evangelicals should be warned that basing their own beliefs upon subjective experiences can result in shipwrecking their own faith in times of storms. Therefore, we do not promote ourselves or our experiences, but rather the authoritative testimony of eyewitnesses as the proof of Christianity and Jesus Christ as the way, the truth, and the life unto salvation.

---

14. Wimber, *Kingdom Evangelism*, 31.

Reasons for a Creedal Apologetic

A creedal apologetic works because it aids the Christian by supporting what they believe and the reasons why as well as guiding them to remain on the important points in discussions with unbelievers. Creedal apologetics keeps the believer grounded and helps remove obstacles that the unbeliever may throw in the path on the way to becoming a Christian. Creedal apologetics reinforces what the Christian believes building them up in our most holy faith as well. A creedal apologetic moves believers off their own "testimony," which is quite subjective, and back onto the solid ground of objective truth.

Focusing on the three parts of the Apostles' Creed keeps us steady when our faith is questioned, our answers scorned and mocked, and those of other religions share their own testimony (subjective) or reasons they believe what they do. Keeping on point with the objective truths formulated and brought together in the Apostles' Creeds helps restrain us from answering tertiary questions or getting off track. The point of apologetics, after all, is to answer their objections, remove the obstacles to belief and proclaim Jesus Christ as the one who died, was buried, and rose again on the third day according to Scripture.

In the "Notes from Concordia in the Larger Catechism Part 2: The Apostles' Creed" it says the following:

> The Ten commandments show us what we are and are not to do, but the Creed shows us the One who creates, redeems, and sanctifies us.[15]

This is the purpose of apologetics within the context of evangelism. Apologetics is not primarily about argument or debate, though that is a part. The chief focus, of which the Apostles' Creed helps us, is to bring the gospel of Jesus Christ to the lost, the sinner, and the person in spiritual crisis. As Christians proclaiming the faith, we will come upon questions about why we believe what it is that we believe and how do we know what we believe is true. Creedal apologetics, by its very name (Latin *credo*) means to believe. It offers to the world a solid, simple, scriptural answer to their questions and skepticism. Anyone sharing and proclaiming the faith is going to come upon those with questions and each of us needs to be prepared to answer for our faith, as the apostle Peter stated when he wrote,

---

15. Dau, *Concordia*, 398.

> But in your hearts honor Christ the Lord as holy, always being prepared to make a defense to anyone who asks you for a reason for the hope that is in you; yet do it with gentleness and respect, having a good conscience, so that, when you are slandered, those who revile your good behavior in Christ may be put to shame. (1 Pet 3:15–16)

Christians who know what we believe and why we believe honor Christ in their hearts. Through the reading and studying of Scripture we prepare ourselves to give an *apologia* (Greek for "answer" or "defense") to anyone, any age, any stage of life, any social position or educational level. We are not reasoning with them intellectually but cutting to the heart of the matter: their spiritual condition as lost sinners in need of forgiveness. We, as Peter says, answer for the "hope that is in you." In this world of pain, misery, death and sin, no one else has a true answer and none but the Christian has true hope.

Often, Christians will begin with the beliefs of their church. That is not where we are to start. Denominations come and go but Christ is eternal. his word is faithful and true. While as a Lutheran I believe we have the best, the most solid exposition of the Scriptures, I am not called to present the Lutheran Church—Missouri Synod but Jesus Christ to sinners. I will invite them to come to my church or find a similar one where they live, but first they must come to Jesus Christ, Savior of sinners, Redeemer of mankind, Destroyer of death and Giver of life eternal. The mistake is made when we present our denomination over and above the gospel. Scripture says that the gospel is the power of God unto salvation (Rom 1:17).

In the letter to the Corinthians, Paul tells them not to argue over who brought them the gospel, or which house they attend for worship (cf. 1 Cor 1:10–16). Instead he reminds them the power of God is in the cross of Christ through the word of God, by which people are being saved (cf. 1 Cor 1:17–18). Therefore, as Dr. Montgomery has reminded students repeatedly, we are not to defend our denomination or denominational peculiarities but the Christian faith. What better way than to utilize the tool the ancient church used to both teach new believers the key parts of the Christian faith and also how to respond to the skeptics? The Apostles' Creed brings out the fullness of the gospel in a simple and matter-of-fact format which can be quickly utilized to proclaim and defend the Christian faith.

As a student of both apologetics and church history I have found that Christians today tend to try to re-invent the wheel. Why? If a tool is already provided, which has worked with skeptics, atheists, pagans, and religious zealots of other faiths, why try to design a new way to offer an apologetic when one already exists? As you will come to see, the church has stood on evidentiary grounds, as expressed in the New Testament for the claims of Jesus of Nazareth, and put them in a simple form, the Apostles' Creed to aid in proclaiming the life, death and resurrection of Jesus to the world around.

In my research I have found a few others who wrote about the creeds and their importance to apologetics, but none laid out a step-by-step guide or how-to so that believers of every age can answer the questions about Christianity. This book is a rubber-hits-the-road type of style. I will go through the history of the Apostles' Creed, its foundation in the Scriptures, and give examples of how to utilize each section.

This book is broken down into each of the three Sections which Martin Luther set up in his Larger Catechism and focuses properly on each person of the Holy Trinity: Father, Son, and Holy Spirit, with regards to answering for the Christian faith. Evidence for the Christian faith is found in the Scriptures and easily remembered when one memorizes the Apostles' Creed. This places a very useful tool in your evangelism toolbox and can be fitted for whatever topic may arise in your discussions with unbelievers. This simple three-part approach should enable you, the Christian, to respond in simplicity and truth to the skeptics' questions.

CHAPTER 2

First Things First

How Do You Know It's True?

THIS IS THE QUESTION so many ask when you are discussing anything from politics to religion. It is the question we should be most prepared to answer when they ask how we know our religion/faith is true and not any other.

As Christians, while our testimony may be a good starting point we cannot stay on that. Why? You cannot prove subjective experience. They may have similar experiences and without objective evidence it breaks down to opinion instead of facts. When one compares the gospels to other ancient documents with regard to their bibliography it becomes evident that we have an overabundance of support for the validity and accuracy as well as the reliability of the gospel accounts.

The importance of the overwhelming number of manuscript copies cannot be overstated. If the same tests for bibliography that are used for other ancient manuscripts are then applied to the gospel and New Testament texts, the gospels are proven beyond a shadow of a doubt to be authentic and reliable. Sir Frederic G. Kenyon states that

> besides number, the manuscripts of the New Testament differ from those of the classical authors . . . In no other case is the interval of time between the composition of the book and the date of the earliest extant manuscripts so short as in that of the New Testament . . . the interval then between the dates of the original composition and the earliest extant evidence becomes so small as to be in fact negligible, and the last foundation for any doubt that the Scriptures have come down to us substantially as they were written has now been removed.[1]

1. Kenyon, *Bible and Archaeology*, 5.

Another authority on the Scriptures is F. F. Bruce and he writes:

> There is no body of ancient literature in the world which enjoys such a wealth of good textual attestation as the New Testament.[2]

In fact, the quotations from the New Testament documents are so numerous and widespread that if we were to lose the manuscripts, the New Testament writings could be reproduced by the writings of the apostolic fathers alone. When one compares the quotes from the early fathers with the writings from the manuscripts it becomes evident that what has come down to us as the inspired word of God has been maintained in its original form; there is no redaction or editing that can be verified but instead the integrity of the original words are maintained. Sir David Dalrymple stated that he had "found the entire New Testament except eleven verses"[3] in the writings of the early church fathers. From the writings and materials that Dean Brugon compiled we have over eighty-five thousand quotations from the New Testament written by the patristic fathers. Based upon the above evidence from bibliographical, internal, and external tests, which is really barely scratching the surface of all the evidence we do have, one can conclude that the New Testament is amply proven to be valid and accurate.

With regards to the internal test one must, as Professor John Warwick Montgomery states, still follow Aristotle's dictum that "the benefit of the doubt is to be given to the document itself, not arrogated by the critic to himself."[4] Paul, in writing to the Corinthians expresses to them that his own office of apostle was validated before them through signs, wonders and miracles (cf. 2 Cor 12:12). This would have been ludicrous on the part of Paul if he wasn't speaking the truth. This second letter to the Corinthians was written to those whom he had ministered personally and could have easily been refuted by the Corinthians themselves if Paul had been lying.

When Paul stood before King Agrippa and gave testimony to the validity of the Christian faith he expressed that all these things, the life of Jesus, the crucifixion, death, and burial and even the resurrection were not "done in a corner."[5] Once again, if the apostle had been lying surely King Agrippa would have stated that at Paul's trial. However, King Agrippa doesn't deny the testimony of Paul but is nearly persuaded by it. These few

---

2. Bruce, *Books and the Parchments*, 178.
3. Leach and Torrey, *Our Bible*, 35.
4. Montgomery, *Faith Founded on Fact*, 96.
5. Sproul, *Reformation Study Bible*, Acts 26:26.

instances show that the internal test for integrity within the New Testament documents remains intact and is passed.

When the New Testament is brought to the bar of the external test for accuracy, faithfulness, and integrity one is forced to face an abundance of evidence once again. The question to be answered by the external test is whether or not other historical materials confirm or deny the internal testimony provided by the documents themselves. With regard to the integrity of the New Testament documents and manuscripts the weight of evidence is on the side of the validity of these documents. One can compare the patristic citations of Scripture as witnesses both to the compilation of documents that have come down to us as the inspired word of God as well as the very words themselves.

God has authenticated his written word in four ways:

- Miracle: The resurrection
- Prophecy: The Old Testament testifies to the New Testament faith as Jesus has fulfilled them
- "Subjective Immediacy":[6] Inner experience. However, first it is the experiences of the evangelists given in their written testimony which we call the New Testament. Then it is our own experience of salvation.
- Natural Theology: This is the evidence from Nature and Creation which is found in the Psalms and primarily in Romans 1 and 2. However, this argument may only convince an unbeliever that there is a god but it will never teach the Gospel which is necessary as the power of God unto salvation.

Personal Experience as Proof

Rather than looking at what the Scriptures say, Evangelicals will go by their gut, their intuition, and state that God is telling them what to do or say. Many in the earliest years of this movement made this subjective word their guiding light. Early Pentecostals defined their movement as rethinking "the Christian faith in light of their new experience of God"[7] rather than on the objective written word. Instead of the Christian faith

---

6. Montgomery, *Defending the Biblical Gospel*.
7. Jacobsen, *Thinking in the Spirit*, ix.

being founded upon objective truth and eyewitness testimony, it is based upon the experiences of the individual.

In a journal note from a personal conversation on February 21, 2004, under the teaching of a former paster of mine, Pastor Rogers (who considers himself to be a modern apostle) reminded me that testimonies are great but you need to invite them to "come and see" for themselves. They need to experience Jesus through visions, dreams, and the anointing they receive. To prove to them Jesus is the Way they must experience him in their personal lives through the anointing (modern-day prophets, seers, and visions).[8] Pastor Rogers taught, "They will not remain Christians for long if God does not excite them to follow him through these various anointing."[9] Without experiences, the modern evangelical holds that the proclamation of the gospel is hindered. They also believe that without miracles and ecstatic/charismatic experiences, the effect of that proclamation will eventually fade away. Without excitements and personal experiences, those who once believed will fall away.

This idea that truth is established through personal experiences and feelings must be challenged. If the gospel is about how you felt one day, and the next day you don't feel or experience it, then the gospel is nothing more than fairy tales which one grows out of. This emphasis on experience, in a gospel presentation, results in its effectiveness being based upon the individual rather than the gospel, which God says "is the power of God unto salvation" (Rom 1:16). It is not experience, though certainly we all do personally experience forgiveness and grace, but it is based upon objective truth which results in sinners being declared justified. It is the notion which both Martin Luther and later CFW Walter expressed as an *inter nos* focus versus *extra nos* focus.

Douglas Jacobsen, in his study of early Pentecostals, says that they had "theological adaptability"[10] and were "creative thinkers who knew how to turn a theological phrase."[11] He writes that because of these two key elements Pentecostalism was able to spread globally and influence people and churches. With an American innovator mentality, these preachers

---

8. Pastor Rogers, sermon titled "Come Unto Jesus," personal journal notes (February 11, 2004).
9. Rogers, "Come Unto Jesus."
10. Jacobsen, *Thinking in the Spirit*, x.
11. Jacobsen, *Thinking in the Spirit*, 11.

were "intent on doing their own thing in their own way."[12] They "took up the task of thinking in the Spirit—of re-reading the Bible in light of their own experiences."[13] For early Pentecostals what mattered was their own experience. Jacobsen summarizes this issue by saying "The one thing that mattered was that the whole thing rang true to their own lived experience of faith and the lived faith of others . . . opting for religious experience"[14] over the written word.

Harvey Cox wrote in *Fire from Heaven*,

> As a theologian I had grown accustomed to studying religious movements by reading what their theologians wrote and trying to grasp the central ideas and the most salient doctrines. But I soon found out that with Pentecostalism this approach does not help much. As one Pentecostal scholar put it, in his faith: "The experience of God has absolute primacy over dogma and doctrine." Therefore the only theology that can give an account of this experience, he says, is a "narrative theology whose central expression is the testimony."[15]

This brings with it great defects to the presentation of the Gospel testimony. If the believer is to proclaim some experience within (*inter nos*) over and against the testimony of Scripture (*extra nos*), the results are debilitating. For the believer those feelings change all the time. No one, if they are honest, feels "saved" all the time. The struggle with sin alone from within and without brings damning charges. Saint Paul even writes about them when he cries out, "Who will deliver me" (Rom 7:24). The world, the devil, and our sinful self constantly contradict us when we rely upon experiences as the foundation we stand on for assurance. If, then, believers who rely upon subjective experiences cannot be sure of their salvation, how will any to whom we proclaim this subjective religion ever be assured that their sins are forgiven and that they too will live eternally? They cannot.

A religion based upon experience and personal testimony "over dogma and doctrine"[16] will either result in pride or depression. If based and kept by pride, pride in one's testimony and experiences, they will fall. However, most believers who based their assurance on their experience

---

12. Jacobsen, *Thinking in the Spirit*, xiii.
13. Jacobsen, *Thinking in the Spirit*, xiii.
14. Jacobsen, *Thinking in the Spirit*, 6.
15. Cox, *Fire from Heaven*, 71.
16. Jacobsen, *Thinking in the Spirit*, 6.

will, in fact, at some point begin to question their salvation and struggle with spiritual depression. All religions based upon an experiential model results in requiring things to obey the law and to keep up with the next anointing and experience. It destroys assurance of faith and calls into question the reality of justification by faith alone based upon the resurrection of Jesus. It stands on a faulty foundation laid in emotions which can be manipulated. Whereas the truth of the gospel, in its properly proclaimed form, is based upon eyewitness testimony validated by fulfilled prophecies of the Old Testament saints according to Scripture.

This idea that experience permeates a gospel presentation is not limited to the early Pentecostals or the latter charismatics and Third Wave movement but continues today. In a series titled "Come Unto Jesus (Part Three)," Pastor Rogers (formerly assistant pastor at Evangel Church, Long Island City, NY) taught that "The Church has focused too much on Christ as Priest and the topics of forgiveness of sin, salvation, grace etc." Furthermore, he infers that when Jesus preached the Gospel of the kingdom He performed miracles, deliverances and healings and so must we.

Once again I stress that the personal experience and testimony of individual believers is a part of Gospel proclamation. However, because people in all other religions also have some type of experiential encounter with their own message, personal testimony becomes a weak argument. Who is to say that what you experienced is based upon objective truth and their testimony is not? How does one know unless they bring in eyewitness testimony which has also been through rigorous review, both by the documented evidence and historical underpinnings? When evangelizing the unbeliever or skeptic, the Christian is engaged both in proclamation and explanation. If either is based upon your own personal experience then unbelievers and skeptics alike may rightfully challenge your message and walk away without believing and being saved.

Two effects of a subjective religion are pride and despair. They are polar opposites between which the pendulum swings for those whose belief in Jesus is based upon subjective experiences or unverifiable claims. It leaves the church in two camps: the haves and the have nots. When objective truth is realized and the eyewitness testimony of the Scriptures elevated to its rightful place, that pendulum begins to find its center on Jesus Christ who lived, died was buried and rose again according to the Scriptures.

If God's word is true, and objectively so, then it is true for all peoples in all times. However, if God's word is subjectively true, then what right or reason do we have for telling others that Jesus is the way, the truth and the life. If it is only based upon subjective experiences, personal opinions and fluttering hearts or goosebumps on our arms, how do we as Christians have the audacity to tell others what they must believe. What is being asked to be believed in? Should they count the cost in following Jesus because of your subjective experience? The objective gospel of which we have the authenticated eyewitness reports is what they should believe: Matthew, Mark, Luke, John and the Acts of the Apostles.

Christianity is objective while all other religions are subjective. Subjective religion puts the burden of being saved and staying saved on the believer. When those hearing the gospel are only hearing about the speaker's personal experiences, it elevates the story of the speaker/preacher to the point where unless those feelings are duplicated in the life of the hearer they may determine that they are either not saved, or lack true faith. The cost of proclaiming one's own experiences and feelings, a subjective proclamation, is to diminish the belief of the other. It creates a two-tiered group of believers: those who have experienced something more and those who have simply believed or have, as Moreland states, "mere Christianity."[17]

Jesus also warned that signs and wonders would not be the norm, would not be given except for one: resurrection.

> Then some of the scribes and Pharisees answered him, saying, "Teacher, we wish to see a sign from you." But he answered them, "An evil and adulterous generation seeks for a sign, but no sign will be given to it except the sign of the prophet Jonah. For just as Jonah was three days and three nights in the belly of the great fish, so will the Son of Man be three days and three nights in the heart of the earth. (Matt 12:38–40)
>
> An evil and adulterous generation seeks for a sign, but no sign will be given to it except the sign of Jonah." So he left them and departed. (Matt 16:4)
>
> When the crowds were increasing, he began to say, "This generation is an evil generation. It seeks for a sign, but no sign will be given to it except the sign of Jonah. For as Jonah became a sign to the people of Nineveh, so will the Son of Man be to this generation. (Luke 11:29–30)

In each of the Scripture passages quoted above the crowds were growing because they saw the miraculous. Jesus was healing and delivering

---

17. Moreland, *Kingdom Triangle*, 172.

people from disease and the demonic, raising some from the dead, and yet he says that an adulterous generation is interested in this. He says that a single sign will be given to them: he will rise from the dead. This is the sign we Christians are to point to because it satisfies the arguments for Christianity and brings in a strong case which can knock down the reasons unbelievers put up against believing the message.

If we discount the power of the word of God, how then can we ever appeal to it for life and godliness, let alone as the witness to the resurrection? By rejecting that God works through this means of grace, we reject the most effective tool God has given us for evangelism and for explaining and defending the Christian faith. Focusing on our own experience will never equate with the power of a simple gospel proclamation based upon the eyewitness testimony of the evangelists. Emphasizing the mere words of Scripture will result in people coming to faith in Christ Jesus.

James Sire writes in his book *Humble Apologetics* that there are several arguments to defend the faith:

1. the case from Jesus,
2. the historical reliability of the gospels,
3. internal coherence of the Christian worldview,
4. the exclusivity of the Christian faith, and
5. personal experience of God.

In making the case from Jesus, Sire writes that the strongest case Christians have for the faith are the words of Jesus himself.[18] Indeed, this is the argument which C. S. Lewis makes regarding Jesus's claims about himself:

> I am trying here to prevent anyone saying the really foolish thing that people often say about Him [that is, Christ]: "I'm ready to accept Jesus as a great moral teacher, but I don't accept His claim to be God." That is the one thing we must not say. A man who was merely a man and said the sort of things Jesus said would not be a great moral teacher. He would either be a lunatic—on a level with the man who says he is a poached egg—or else he would be the devil of Hell. You must make your choice. Either this man was, and is, the Son of God: or else a madman or something worse.... You can shut Him up for a fool, you can spit at Him and kill Him

---

18. Sire, *Little Primer on Humble Apologetics*, 73.

as a demon; or you can fall at His feet and call Him Lord and God. But let us not come up with any patronizing nonsense about His being a great human teacher. He has not left that open to us. He did not intend to.[19]

It is the gospel testimony which has converted so many throughout the two thousand years since the resurrection and should not ever be relegated to a tertiary or even secondary position behind one's own experiences or testimony. Instead, the gospel must be at the front of our evangelistic message and explanation as to its truth. By pointing the unbeliever or skeptic to the written gospel texts, we truly introduce them to Jesus and the saving grace found in him through his word.

There are other issues that come from a focus on a subjective message, of personal revelations and experiences over and against the written word of God. Each of these issues debilitates the defense and proclamation of the gospel because it diminishes the importance of that word. We do well to follow the path and pattern (as will be shown in the next chapter) which the apostles and Paul used: Jesus died, was buried, and rose again according to the Scriptures. The message we have must be based upon these truths because from start to finish it is creedal: I believe.

Defending the Objective Word of God

> You should not believe your conscience and your feelings more than the Word which the Lord who receives sinners preaches to you.[20] —Martin Luther

Christianity is an objective religion. Christianity bases its proof on the eyewitness testimony of the physical resurrection of Jesus Christ. If this historical and documented event did not actually occur in the personal knowledge of the Evangelists, they themselves declare that we would be most pitied among all other religions. Throughout this chapter it will be shown how other religions are based upon the subjective, so when Evangelicals adopt this pattern they weaken and ruin the proclamation of the gospel, debilitating it before the world.

If the gospel is subjectively true only if I feel something or experience God, how can it ever be verified? In dealing with the subjective origins of

---

19. Lewis, *Mere Christianity*, 52.
20. Althaus, *Theology of Martin Luther*, 59.

other religions and cults of Christianity, it will be explored how feelings, experiences, and personal opinion brought about false religions. A comparison with cults of Christianity will also be made to show how using a subjective basis for proof in Pentecostalism mirrors that of these heresies. As previously stated, two other religions and one cult will be used to demonstrate how Pentecostalism is no similar to these false worldviews and therefore leaves the Christian witness damaged and crippled.

Any Christian witness that explains the gospel apart from God's written word will end badly because it inevitably places the feelings and experience of the individual above Scripture. This is what happens in other religions and cults. When this method is used it ignores the fact that God has given us objective truth in his special revelation we call the Bible. This is also true when modern Evangelicals rely upon feelings and emotions to bring people into the faith. Their basis of truth is no different than that of other religions. For example, a Mormon will typically tell you to pray about it and you'll feel the burning of the bosom. How is this different than the excitements in a Evangelical service as evidence by running, rolling on the floor, shouting in incomprehensible sounds, or hearing voices in your own head? It is not. The purpose of this chapter is to show the fallacy of basing a gospel presentation on subjective feelings or experiences.

We do not promote ourselves or our experiences but the authoritative testimony of eyewitnesses as the proof of Christianity and Jesus Christ as the way, the truth, and the life unto salvation. Therefore, our defense must be a creedal apologetic

Our Creed Is the Gospel, *Not* Our Experience

Experience is insufficient to be what you believe. Experience is *not* your creed. The message of believers to unbelievers, seekers, or skeptics must be Jesus Christ and him crucified. We must say, along with the apostles, him we proclaim. Experiences come and go. Experiences change and vary one believer to the next. Experience, because it is subjective, is quite the slippery slope to stand on. What God has given his church is a sure word which withstands every assault against it.

Believers everywhere, whether Pentecostal, charismatic, Calvinist, Baptist, or Lutheran, must proclaim the message God has given us. We have a singular gospel which God gave the church to offer those lost in sin and dying apart from Christ. We can teach the denominational peculiarities of our particular lot later but the most important message is that Jesus lived, died and rose again according to the Scripture. The choice is clear as to how to proclaim and defend and it is through a creedal apologetic.

Just the Facts

Instead, when presenting the objective gospel it must be emphasized repeatedly that the Christian faith is objective. In this aspect it stands head and shoulders above and beyond every single other religion.

Apologetics can help remove obstacles to faith and thus aid unbelievers in embracing the gospel. Certainly the Holy Spirit must be involved in drawing men to Christ. But a preacher is not absolved of the responsibility of preparing his sermon just because the Spirit must apply the word of God to the lives of his listeners. In the same way, ambassadors for Christ are not excused from the responsibility of defending the gospel. The Spirit can use evidence to convict men of the truth of the proclamation.[21]

While the argument is that utilizing any objective defense limits or replaces the work of the Holy Spirit, the Scriptures say differently. The apostle Peter states that when unbelievers or skeptics begin to question not only what we believe, we are to be prepared with an answer (*apologia*) and a defense of the faith. "Have no fear of them, nor be troubled, but in your hearts honor Christ the Lord as holy, always being prepared to make a defense to anyone who asks you for a reason for the hope that is in you" (1 Pet 3:15) Notice how Peter reminds us that in preparing a reason for the hope we have, salvation in Christ from sin, death, and the devil, we "honor Christ." In no way do we supersede the work of the Holy Spirit with learning to defend the faith and then offering that evidence to unbelievers.

Conclusion

We live in a contemporary society which states that everyone has their own truth. From the East we are told that God resides within us. From the West we have Islam which informs us that though they have no eyewitnesses to the events Mohammed wrote about, though many of the original documents were destroyed or copies were burned, we are to believe his message simply because he said it happened. Within the cults we are told to look

---

21. Moreland, *Scaling the Secular City*.

to specific charismatic leaders who have heard the voice of God for themselves. Even, as in the case of Mormonism, though the supposed eyewitnesses recanted, those looking into it are told to read the Book of Mormon and a burning of the bosom will prove their faith true.

The answer to this is that every believer must move quickly from testifying of their own personal experience, away from their own denominational peculiarities and subjective experiences on to the Gospel of Christ and Him Crucified and Risen Again. The reason for defending the faith is to bring the unbeliever to the foot of the cross so that, by the grace of God, they might repent and believe in Him. Believers of all theological backgrounds must focus back onto the Gospel. As Netland writes,

> In our witness to an unbelieving work primacy must always be given the simple, direct, Spirit-anointed proclamation of the Gospel . . . where appropriate, such witness should also be supplemented by informed and sensitive response to criticism and questions and demonstration of why one should accept the claims of Christian faith.[22]

Nowhere are we told that our experiences prove the Christian faith and to do so debilitates a proper Gospel proclamation by relying upon the same faulty ground as every other cult and world religion as argued in the chapter on other religions.

It is the responsibility of the Christian to prove the case for the Christian faith. We are the defense team and the skeptic or religious person is the prosecutor. If we refuse to use the eyewitness testimony given to us in the Scriptures we may lose the case. By giving subjective testimony which says, "I feel it is true because . . ." we relinquish that which is unique to the Christian faith. Only by an objective approach can obstacles be removed one by one along the road to the house of salvation.

Imagine, if you will, the prosecutor demanding evidence of the Christian to prove the case for Christ's resurrection and we simply say, "I believe it to be true because of a vision I had." The skeptic or prosecutor may then rightly call Mohammed or Joseph Smith to the stand. Questioning them, they would testify to a vision and declare their respective religions to then be true. This subjective defense would actually be no defense at all. Christians are called to give a defense (*apologia*) for the faith we have and that is through objective evidence.

---

22. Netland, *Evangelical Apologetics*, 297.

If Christians are to give a defense of the faith it must be done objectively. Offering the world a subjective type of Christianity is actually offering it side by side with any other false religion or cult. Over and over in this thesis it has been emphasized that the Christian faith is an objective and verifiable faith. If Christians, mainly those in Pentecostal and charismatic churches, relinquish this aspect of the faith, we end up surrendering the uniqueness of Christianity. Every other religion is based upon subjective experience, hearsay accounts, and many through personal and private revelations. Only Christianity stands mountains above with objective truth and it behooves all to rely upon the evidences given by God to the church of in all times and all places.

Sir Norman Anderson writes about "the unique proclamation of the apostolic church and the ways in which it differs from that of other faith."[23]

> We saw that the apostles concentrated on recounting, again and again, a historical event which was intimately known to them, and to which they could give their unqualified, personal testimony; the life, words and deeds, and above all the death and resurrection , of One with whom they had kept close company for some three years . . . they could not be silenced from "speaking about what we have seen and heard" (Acts 4:20).[24]

We do not proclaim our subjective experiences, our personal revelations, our private and direct conversations with God, or our feelings about the faith. Instead, we are to focus on Christ who is the center and circumference of our faith. The objective approach is the only one which proactively removes the hurdles the nonbeliever uses to deny the validity of the gospel.

Therefore, our defense of the Christian faith must be a creedal apologetic.

---

23. Anderson, *Christianity and World Religions*, 176.
24. Anderson, *Christianity and World Religions*, 176.

CHAPTER 3

Creeds in the Bible?

Biblical and Beneficial

DID YOU KNOW THERE are ancient creeds in the Bible? Short statements of faith passed down from believer to believer, generation to generation? Those in more liturgical churches will be familiar with the Three Ecumenical Creeds, Apostles, Nicene and Athanasian; how many in modern evangelical churches know these? Moreover, how many Christians knew that there are creedal statements in the Bible? Don't worry, I did not know this either until I began to study church history and the creeds. In this chapter, I will be reviewing the creedal statements made in the Bible, from the Old and New Testaments, to show that there is a Scriptural precedent for "I believe" statements. Keep your Bible handy along with a notebook so you can jot these down and commit them to memory. Remember that the Apostles' Creed, which is the belief statement focused on in this book, relies upon the word of God for its truth statements. So, as we go through these, keep a copy of the Apostles' Creed (provided in the appendix of this book) nearby to annotate in order to review them should questions arise.

Far from creeds being something imposed upon believers or being unbiblical, throughout the word of God we find creedal statements and confessions. Rev. Daniel Hyde, in his article "Creeds and Confessions," writes that they are not merely Roman Catholic traditions nor do they stifle the work of the Holy Spirit.[1]

We live in a time when objective truth is questioned and subjective ideas flourish. Objectivity is suspicious and relegated to the past. Today, our feelings are honored more than facts. This places the church in a strange position. Many modern evangelicals, and Christians of historical

---

1. Hyde, "Creeds and Confessions."

churches, are moving away from creedal statements, instead replacing them with personal testimonies. Confessing the creeds on Sunday morning is removed and a "time for testimony" is given. The subjective is overtaking objective truth as the world tells us and pressures us to join them in their feelings and experiences.

However, Christianity has always been a creedal religion. From the earliest records in the New Testament, we are given statements of faith. These are more "I-pass-on-as-I-received" or "delivered to you . . . " and tend to be in poetical and hymn-like formulas. Music has a tendency to enable us to remember things better. If I would say "Let earth receive her King" you might immediately think of the Christmas hymn "Joy to the World." A study in Finland found that cognitive brain power was improved by putting information to music.[2] Another found that music improved the cognitive skills and memory retention in patients with dementia.[3] Scripture, thousands of years before these studies, and before Mozart himself was born, had already put the teachings of God to music in what we call the Psalms. Imagine learning Psalm 119 just by memorizing it word-for-word. Now, picture it put to a tune easily learned and you will have memorization of Scripture using the "Mozart Effect."[4]

In the same way, poetry is retained in the memory quite quickly. A recent study (1995[5]) on the effect of poetic form in memory retention found this:

> Poems and songs often emphasize the sound patterns, or form, of words. Across centuries and cultures, stories have been transformed into poems and songs that are subsequently memorized and passed on without the aid of written references. One explanation of this remarkable feat of memory is that sound patterns provide salient organizational frameworks for lyrical material (Rubin, 1995). When portions of a lyrical piece are forgotten, form-based structures may serve as reference points to cue memory.[6]

Thus, the New Testament writers' habit of using poetic and hymnal form, in the original languages, enabled the essentials of the faith to come back to memory much more quickly and easily. This also made for easier

2. Klemm, "Does Music Help Memory?," paras. 5–8.
3. Paul, "How Music Can Improve Memory."
4. Atchley and Hare, "Memory for Poetry."
5. Rubin, *Memory in Oral Traditions*.
6. Atchley and Hare, "Memory for Poetry," 1.

and better memorizing. In the appendix is a list of resources to sing the Apostles' Creed and memorize it.

The apostle John reminds the church (2 John 1) that they are to abide in the word of Christ. This is a confessional exhortation. He is reminding them that the truths which have been spoken by Jesus, passed down through the apostles, are to be remembered. However, not only should they know these truths, what is to be believed (Latin *credo*) but abide in them, keeping them and not going elsewhere for some other truth. These teachings, codified in the early creeds and confessions, which Saint Paul reminds us were passed down from the apostles to the churches throughout the world, were to be believed upon and anyone with something different was not even to be permitted entry to the local church (which met in homes as in the case of the church Saint John writes to in this letter).

> Everyone who goes on ahead and does not abide in the teaching of Christ, does not have God. Whoever abides in the teaching has both the Father and the Son. ¹⁰ If anyone comes to you and does not bring this teaching, do not receive him into your house or give him any greeting. (2 John 9–10)

So, let us look at the creeds, statements of "I believe" or "delivered to you" which the church from Abraham to the end of this age, have and are to continue to confess and abide by. Since many contemporary evangelicals, Pentecostals/charismatics and nondenominational churches have a tendency to reject the early church creeds, it is my desire that they see the precedent set in the Scriptures, continued through by the disciples of the apostles and their disciples as well. A comment will be made after each Scripture so that the reader may see the main doctrine it is teaching and compare that with the Apostles' Creed which is our pattern, in this book, for a creedal apologetic.

Old Testament Creeds

> Hear, O Israel: The LORD our God, the LORD is one. (Deut 6:4)

This is known as the Shema ("hear") which is the first word in the Hebrew. It is an early creed of the people of God, Israel of old, which speaks of the fact that there is one God and not many like in other religions (and the Canaanite land they were going to enter). Jews still recite this as a prayer daily and is taught diligently to their children as it has from generation to generation.

Ambrose said this verse reminds us that God is "unchangeable, always abiding in unity of power, always the same, and not altered by any accession or diminution."[7] As Christians we hold that God is One who has revealed himself in the three persons of the Trinity: Father, Son, and Holy Spirit. The unity of the Godhead is echoed in the Old Testament with plural terms used for the name of God, as in Genesis 1:26 recounting of God saying, "Let *us* make man in *our* image" (emphasis added):

> When you come into the land that the LORD your God is giving you for an inheritance and have taken possession of it and live in it, you shall take some of the first of all the fruit of the ground, which you harvest from your land that the LORD your God is giving you, and you shall put it in a basket, and you shall go to the place that the LORD your God will choose, to make his name to dwell there. And you shall go to the priest who is in office at that time and say to him, "I declare today to the LORD your God that I have come into the land that the LORD swore to our fathers to give us." Then the priest shall take the basket from your hand and set it down before the altar of the LORD your God.
>
> And you shall make response before the LORD your God, "A wandering Aramean was my father. And he went down into Egypt and sojourned there, few in number, and there he became a nation, great, mighty, and populous. And the Egyptians treated us harshly and humiliated us and laid on us hard labor. Then we cried to the LORD, the God of our fathers, and the LORD heard our voice and saw our affliction, our toil, and our oppression. And the LORD brought us out of Egypt with a mighty hand and an outstretched arm, with great deeds of terror, with signs and wonders. And he brought us into this place and gave us this land, a land flowing with milk and honey. And behold, now I bring the first of the fruit of the ground, which you, O LORD, have given me." And you shall set it down before the LORD your God and worship before the LORD your God. And you shall rejoice in all the good that the LORD your God has given to you and to your house, you, and the Levite, and the sojourner who is among you. (Deut 26:1–11)

In this passage are the instructions to the Israelites of what they are to confess when they come to bring offerings and sacrifices to the altar of the

---

7. Schaff, *Select Library*, 10:150.

LORD. This confession of faith was to be repeated every time they brought sacrifices to God. They were also expected to teach this confession to their children and pass it down from generation to generation. This creedal confession recounts the might and provision of God as they wandered before He brought them to the land promised to Abraham and their forefathers. They were never to forget His goodness and the right He had to their offerings and first fruits from their harvests. They were to worship God alone and extend this kindness to the stranger as well living out the mercy they were confessing in this passage.

> And when all the people saw it, they fell on their faces and said, "The LORD, he is God; the LORD, he is God." (1 Kgs 18:39)

This is the confession of faith which Israel gave after the confrontation between the prophets of Baal whom Ahab followed and that of Elijah the prophet of the God of Israel. The people were following the false prophets of Baal and God instructed Elijah to confront them. The false prophets began to sacrifice to their gods and the only stipulation was that no one could actually light the fire, their god/gods had to do that. After a very long time, and some teasing by Elijah towards the false prophets, they gave up.

Elijah then instructs them to dig a trench around the sacrifice and fill it with water to overflowing. He prays a very short prayer and fire consumes not only the animal but the wood and stones, and licks up every last drop of water. The people, realizing the folly of their sins, immediately repent and confess that the LORD, he is God. This becomes a creed, a statement that we believe in the one true God, the LORD.

New Testament Creeds

In the New Testament alone, we find over a dozen creedal statements. That is quite an amount to simply dispute or disregard. The apostles were passing down statement of faith, creedal declarations before many of the books and letters of the New Testament were even written because it was important to instruct the new in the faith in the teachings of Jesus. Just as, in the Old Testament, Israel was taught to pass down the Ten Commandments and other creedal statements to their children, the apostles (who were brought up under that educational system) would have done the same. In each of these statements we find that the central fact is this: Jesus is the Christ and must be believed in. It is important to remember that creeds, whether written by the apostles or the early church leaders, are a simplified way to remember the essential teachings of the Christian church.

Gospel Creeds

> Simon Peter replied, "You are the Christ, the Son of the living God." (Matt 16:16)

One of the very first creeds we find in the New Testament is right in the middle section of the first gospel, that of Matthew. This is a pivotal section and marks the climax of the teaching section of this gospel from chapters four to sixteen. Earlier, in 11:2–3, John the Baptist asked Jesus, "Are you the one who is to come, or shall we look for another?" Jesus's response is to list the evidences given in the prophets which believers were to look for to authenticate he is the Messiah (Anointed One), the Christ, Son of the Living God. Now, Peter is boldly confessing that Jesus is that promised Messiah and the One who is to come.

> And he asked them, "But who do you say that I am?" Peter answered him, "You are the Christ." (Mark 8:29)

What is fascinating about this event is that it can be found in all three of the Synoptic Gospels.[8] That gives this statement extra weight to its importance. Each author of their specific Gospel places this event near the middle of their Gospel accounts, which marks it as a pivotal point in the life of Jesus. Mark opens his Gospel by calling Jesus the Christ, but here in chapter 8 it is the disciples who now understand Jesus is the Messiah and confess it.

> Then he said to them, "But who do you say that I am?" And Peter answered, "The Christ of God." (Luke 9:20)

Here we read that Luke also writes of this event and it is placed near the middle of his Gospel account; as Luke said, he diligently searched out the truth from those who walked with Jesus (Luke 1:1–4). While the disciples believed Jesus to be a teacher, using the term "Rabbi," here now Peter boldly confesses that Jesus is more than that; Jesus is the Messiah, the Christ of God. No longer is following Jesus as a good teacher enough, but one must

---

8. Matthew, Mark and Luke are called the Synoptic Gospels because of the similarities in timeline, events, and identical statements found in all three. The Gospel of John has a distinct focus and is not part of the Synoptic Gospels.

confess that he is the Anointed One, the One prophesied of through Moses and the Prophets, the Lord of All sent by God who is himself very God of very God, as the Nicene Creed[9] phrases it.

This creed is of such importance to the Christian faith that each of these three Gospels records the event in detail with great similarity. How much, then, should we also affirm this creed and confess it to all who ask "Who is this Jesus?" We too must say, unequivocally, "Jesus is the Christ, the Son of the Living God." The Apostles' Creed repeats this when through it we confess with the church worldwide, "And in Jesus Christ, his only Son, our Lord."

> Nathanael answered him, "Rabbi, you are the Son of God! You are the King of Israel!" (John 1:49)

Coming to the Gospel of John we find him beginning his account with the words, "In the beginning was the Word and the Word was God." He does not mince words here but boldly proclaims Jesus to be Very God of Very God, the Word made flesh, God incarnate for us. Then we come to the story of Philip, a follower of John the Baptist who witnessed the baptism of Jesus. Philip finds Nathanael and tells him, "We found him of whom Moses in the Law and also the Prophets wrote, Jesus of Nazareth." Nathanael is quite the skeptic, wondering out loud if anything good can come from Nazareth. In Jesus's response to Nathanael we have the first evidence of his divine knowledge, and upon that Nathanael makes this confession which must also be our own: You are the Son of God! You are the King of Israel!

> Simon Peter answered him, "Lord, to whom shall we go? You have the words of eternal life, and we have believed, and have come to know, that you are the Holy One of God." (John 6:68–69)

In John 6 we have a very difficult teaching to both understand and believe. Jesus tells the crowd of five-thousand-plus, whom he'd just miraculously fed, that "unless you eat the flesh of the Son of Man and drink his blood, you have no life in you." The result, as John recounts, is that many of those who had been following Jesus walk away. Jesus then turns to the

---

9. "And in one Lord Jesus Christ, the only begotten Son of God, begotten of His Father before all worlds, God of God, Light of Light, very God of very God, begotten, not made, being of one substance with the Father, by whom all things were made; who for us men and for our salvation came down from heaven and was incarnate by the Holy Spirit of the virgin Mary and was made man." See https://www.lcms.org/about/beliefs/lutheran-confessions to view this creed.

Twelve and asks, "Do you want to go away as well?" Peter's bold response is not only that Jesus's teachings bring life but because of what they have seen and heard they know him to be the Messiah.

There are many more of these confessions in the four Gospels but I will conclude them with this one from Jesus himself:

> And this is eternal life, that they know you, the only true God, and Jesus Christ whom you have sent. (John 17:3)

In what is called Jesus's high priestly prayer, for his disciples as well as all who come to believe in him, Jesus tells us where eternal life is to be found: In him whom God sent into the world. Jesus makes two points in this confession:

To Know God Is to Have Eternal Life

You must know and believe in Jesus because true knowledge is inseparable from God in Christ.

Here Jesus shows that he is of the Father's nature; and he has given us to know that of the True Father he is the True Offspring. Jesus added himself to the Father teaching that they are One. Only those who confess this fact are true believers and have eternal life. The Athanasian Creed goes into great detail about the unity of the Godhead and rightly says that unless this is believed you are not in the Faith:

> Now this is the catholic faith:
> That we worship one God in trinity and the trinity in unity,
> neither blending their persons
> nor dividing their essence.
> For the person of the Father is a distinct person,
> the person of the Son is another,
> and that of the Holy Spirit still another.
> But the divinity of the Father, Son, and Holy Spirit is one,
> their glory equal, their majesty coeternal . . .
>
> Anyone then who desires to be saved
> should think thus about the trinity.
> But it is necessary for eternal salvation
> that one also believe in the incarnation

of our Lord Jesus Christ faithfully.
Now this is the true faith:
That we believe and confess
that our Lord Jesus Christ, God's Son,
is both God and human, equally.
He is God from the essence of the Father,
begotten before time;
and he is human from the essence of his mother,
born in time;
completely God, completely human,
with a rational soul and human flesh;
equal to the Father as regards divinity,
less than the Father as regards humanity.
Although he is God and human,
yet Christ is not two, but one.
He is one, however,
not by his divinity being turned into flesh,
but by God's taking humanity to himself.
He is one,
certainly not by the blending of his essence,
but by the unity of his person.
For just as one human is both rational soul and flesh,
so too the one Christ is both God and human. (Athanasian Creed, circa 500 AD)

My Lord and my God. —John 20:28

The Athanasian Creed should remind us of the confession of the apostle, Philip Schaff, in his work *The Creeds of Christendom*, the following regarding this confession: "This is the strongest apostolic confession of faith in the Lordship and divinity of Christ."[10] These words are addressed to Jesus Christ and are not an exclamation of astonishment addressed to God. In the latter case Thomas would have uttered a profanity that was under review by Jesus. When Thomas saw the imprint of the nails the ones to the side of Jesus he shouted in praise "My Lord and my God" (John

---

10. Schaff, "Confessiones Ecclesiae Apostolicae," 2:5.

20:28). This again is the confession of faith that every true Christian must have: Jesus is Lord and God over all.

Apostolic Statements of Faith

> And as they were going along the road they came to some water, and the eunuch said, "See, here is water! What prevents me from being baptized?" And Philip said, "If you believe with all your heart, you may." And he replied, "I believe that Jesus Christ is the Son of God." (Acts 8:36–37)

Now we come to the Acts of the Apostles and their own letters/epistles. Perhaps for some, they find it richly interspersed with creeds and confessions given to the church to keep them in the true faith. The first example of a creed is the conversation between the eunuch and Philip, a deacon in the early church. The Ethiopian eunuch was already a Jewish convert, well-versed in and believing the Scriptures, searching them diligently to know more about the one true God but perplexed about the passage he was reading in the Prophet Isaiah. Philip expounds upon the Scriptures and explains that Jesus is the fulfillment of that passage which prophecies about the suffering servant. When the eunuch asks what may prevent him from being baptized, since he believes this message, Philip responds with a part of a confessional statement: if you believe with all your heart (cf. Acts 8:20–46). The eunuch responds with a creedal statement, "I believe that Jesus Christ is the Son of God." This is exactly what Matthew, Mark, and Luke recounted when Peter made the bold confession of faith to Jesus, which was discussed earlier in this chapter. This too must be our creedal statement and the focus of apologetics is to drive the message home that Jesus is the Son of God, the forgiver of all our sins and only through him may we receive eternal life.

Throughout the letters of the apostle Paul we find both short and long creeds and confessional statements which must be held to in order to be of the true faith. Each of these creeds has an apologetic within which we should familiarize ourselves which in order to answer for our faith.

> Concerning his Son, who was descended from David according to the flesh and was declared to be the Son of God in power according to the Spirit of holiness by his resurrection from the dead, Jesus Christ our Lord. (Rom 1:3–4)

As the apostle Paul begins his letter, he gives a formal greeting to the church in Rome. In the third and fourth verse we begin to read a creedal statement chock full of doctrine. He begins with explaining that according to the Scriptures through the promises and prophecies concerning God's own son, Jesus Christ, is descended from the line of King David. This simple creed immediately reminds us that Jesus is God in the flesh come to us in and through the power of God's Spirit. In Romans 1 we find the incarnation. We learn that Jesus is both God and Man, coequal and coeternal. These early church creeds were expressions of faith and modern Christians would benefit from affirming them either in the Scripture or in the early church writings where they agree with God's Holy Word.

The very next thing Paul speaks of is the physical resurrection from the dead. Later in our Bibles but earlier in Paul's writings we find Paul saying that if the resurrection did not happen Christians are to be pitied. Here, in his letter to the Romans, this is the first thing he writes of: the life, death, and resurrection of Jesus, Son of David as far as his humanity is concerned and equally Son of God as for his deity. In Paul's letter to the Corinthian church he tells them that apart from a physical bodily historical and actual resurrection we remain in our sins. This bodily resurrection serves to affirm the deity of Jesus Christ and the completion of saving work in the forgiveness of all of our sins.

Here at the very beginning of Paul's letter to the Romans, we have a statement of faith, an "I believe" and "you believe" statement. This is an early confession of faith and creed: they believe in Jesus raised from the dead. This must be our confession of faith as well, that Jesus Christ has risen from the dead.

> If you confess with your mouth that Jesus is Lord and believe in
> your heart that God raised him from the dead, you will be saved.
> (Rom 10:9)

In this next confession of faith from the book of Romans, the apostle Paul joins two aspects of a single reality to be both confessed and believed. There is no separating these two. If you believe Jesus to be the Son of God descended from David then with your mouth, you make this confession. However, a confession of the mouth that is not believed in the heart is not saving faith but merely mental agreement and is not salvific. Only because the heart has faith, gifted by God through the means of grace, can the verbal confession which says "Jesus is Lord and God raised him from the dead" can possibly be true saving faith. Simply mentally affirming that

Jesus was an actual historical figure, taught people to love God and their neighbor, who died on the cross, without believing the message he taught, or believing he truly rose again from the dead, leaves one outside the one true faith. Paul further shows that everyone who makes this outward confession, believing it in their heart, will be saved.

> Yet for us there is one God, the Father, from whom are all things and for whom we exist, and one Lord, Jesus Christ, through whom are all things and through whom we exist. (1 Cor 8:6)

We now move on to Paul's letter to the Corinthians which is actually one of the earliest, if not the first, of Paul's epistles. In it he gives a confession of the first two persons of the Holy Trinity, "one God, the Father, and one Lord, Jesus Christ, through whom everything exists." What does this passage tell us? It informs us that Jesus was very involved in creation and continues to be the one keeping everything together. This confession of faith enables us to begin answering the questions that an atheist may bring to you. "What is it that you believe about Jesus?" "Was he there at creation?" "Who made this world?" "Why were they created?" and "Were things created or did they just happen?" When we begin to learn the creeds and confessions that are in the Scriptures we become better equipped to answer their questions.

> Therefore I want you to understand that no one speaking in the Spirit of God ever says "Jesus is accursed!" and no one can say "Jesus is Lord" except in the Holy Spirit. (1 Cor 12:3)

Paul has sprinkled throughout his letters several creedal statements and this one, like all the others, is important. Earlier in this chapter when I reviewed the synoptic Gospels about the question Jesus posed to the disciples, "Who do the people say that I am?" (cf. Matt 16), the answer that Peter gave was this: "You are the Christ." Well, here it is again but from the apostle Paul, "Jesus is Lord." This seems to be one of the earliest forms of creed for the ancient church. Paul reminds them that only those whose hearts have been changed can even say this creed truthfully. Only by the power of the Holy Spirit, the Lord and giver of life, can anyone with their heart and mind, confess this creed.

> For I delivered to you as of first importance what I also received: that Christ died for our sins in accordance with the Scriptures, 4 that he was buried, that he was raised on the third day in accordance with the Scriptures. (1 Cor 15:3–4)

We now come to this major creedal statement which the apostle Paul affirms was given to him when he says "received" and begins by saying "I delivered to you." Although Paul had much to teach the Corinthian church nothing mattered above and beyond this truth: Jesus died and rose from the dead. Paul marks this out as first importance. One could say that what follows is the most important doctrine of the Christian church. What is most important? That Jesus Christ died to forgive us of our sins, was buried, and that he raised himself on that third day. All of this was in fulfillment of the prophecies from Moses through to the last of the prophets, Malachi. Everything in the Old Testament Scriptures pointed to Jesus Christ and him crucified, buried, and raised on the third day (see Luke 24). This is a confessional and creedal statement of utmost importance both to know and to be believed. If one does not believe in the actual and physical resurrection from the dead of Jesus of Nazareth, they remain outside the one true faith and without eternal life.

By far this is the creed I turn to nearly every time a question is asked of me about Jesus. So many are taught that Jesus is a good teacher but he is not God. This text is where I plant my feet, dig in, and bring them the evidence for the Christian faith. This, since Scripture says it is "of first importance," is what I focus upon. If they've asked me why I'm a Christian, I get off of my personal testimony and onto the testimony of the evangelists: Jesus died, was buried, and rose again according to the Scriptures. Yet, by using the Apostles' Creed it can be simplified, both for me to remember what is essential, and in phrasing it in a way they may even be familiar with. This is the key to apologetics, removing their stumbling blocks and proclaiming the gospel. Here, in this text we have the gospel so succinctly put: Jesus died for sinners and was raised from the dead.

As the apostle Paul said, this is the most important thing to remember and proclaim. Nothing else matters. This is the gospel message. This is the focus of doing apologetics. This is the central part of any and all conversations with unbelievers. This is the message we are to proclaim. This is the point of apologetics. This is the reason to engage them and answer their questions about the faith. This is the reason we involve ourselves in apologetics. This is the reason we tell them the good news. This is the reason we focus upon the life, death, burial, and resurrection of Jesus because this is "of first importance."

> There is one body and one Spirit—just as you were called to the one hope that belongs to your call—one Lord, one faith, one

> baptism, one God and Father of all, who is over all and through all and in all. (Eph 4:4–6)

Moving through the epistles we come to the creedal statement found in Ephesians, the fourth chapter. Here we have the basic doctrines of the faith Paul begins holding possibly in ancient him. Earlier in this chapter I spoke about how many of the creedal statements and doctrines of the church were formed as early hymns and poems. I repeat: this enables one to better retain what is learned. This confession begins with the church when it talks about one body. Then Paul goes into one spirit meaning the Holy Spirit who unites us all in that one church.

Then we see Paul says "one Lord," which is a confession of Jesus as Jehovah, the one true God. This is what we read in Romans 10:9. Paul continues that we the one body are one faith. Paul is not talking about the act of believing, rather what is believed: true doctrine. Then he continues that there is one baptism. In my book, *The Accidental Lutheran*, I explain how there is one baptism for the forgiveness of sins. This is what Paul is talking about. Many evangelicals believe there are two baptisms, one by the Holy Spirit and another by water. However, that is not what the Scripture teaches. We read here one faith and one baptism. That baptism is your water baptism where Saint Peter writes in his first letter (3:21) that in those baptismal waters with the word we are forgiven. This is the one and only baptism Scripture teaches us.

Paul continues that there is one God and Father of all. This teaches us that there is only one God whom we call Father and Son and Holy Spirit. We are also reminded that God is Father over everyone and everything because he created it all. However only through Jesus Christ can we acknowledge God as our Father. That parent-child relationship with God only comes through faith in God the Son, Jesus Christ. In his commentary on Luther's catechsim, Albrecht Peters summarizes Luther's view on this:

> As is demonstrated in the three articles, the twofold way in which the triune God reveals himself separates true Christians from all other human beings. Even though his creatures, the latter may yearn for a relationship with the one Creator God, they remain under the holy God's judgment of wrath for as long a time as God's free grace in Jesus Christ has not yet opened to them through the Spirit.[11]

---

11. Peters, "Luther's Understanding of the Apostles' Creed," 5.

Concordia the Lutheran Confessions says regarding article 1 of the Apostles' Creed in the note that "since God is the maker of heaven and earth, we realize that all we are, all we will ever become, and so we possess depends entirely on our Creator.[12] Luther says in his catechism explanation on the first part of the Apostles' Creed, when discussing God the Father, that only those in Christ "see his fatherly heart and his surpassing love toward us (Exodus 34:6)."[13] What this means is that "since God is Almighty he is able to save me. Since he is father, he will do it." Luther's catechetical sermon of September 21, 1528, explains this very idea that God offers himself throughout the creation and "because he is our father he has poured himself out freely and given us eternal life."[14]

Furthermore, Luther says, "we also confess that God the Father has not only given us all that we have and see before our eyes, but daily preserves and defends us against all evil and misfortune . . . He does all this out of pure love and goodness, without our merit, as a kind father . . . [therefore] we say 'Father Almighty.'"[15] It is here that we see another way to answer those outside the faith: "God is my creator and my father. Who better to know me and my needs, you and your needs, then the one who made you and loved you enough to send his only begotten son into the world to die for your sins and rise again to give you eternal life."

Hymns to Christ as to a God . . . Pliny the Younger

I love church history. It all began when our church back east was invited to a conference in Pennsylvania on Athanasius. The title was "Athanasius Contra Mundo (Athanasius Against the World)" and the keynote speaker was Rev. Carl Truman who was president of Westminster Theological Seminary until his resignation some years later. He was very instrumental in planting an interest, which grew into a love, of church history. As I learned more and more about the church throughout the centuries an appreciation grew for the ancient church and its ongoing battle for the truth. Even when most pastors and bishops were teaching falsehoods, as in the time of Athanasius's battle against the heretic Arius who denied the Trinity, small groups maintained

12. Dau, *Concordia*, 399.
13. Dau, *Concordia*, 401.
14. Peters, "Luther's Understanding of the Apostles' Creed," 61.
15. Dau, *Concordia*, 400.

fidelity to God's word and kept to orthodoxy. This passion lead to reading more and more of the history around the ancient church.

That leads me to a letter, written by a man called Pliny the Younger, which he wrote to his Uncle, Pliny the Elder. Pliny was born Gaius Plinius Caecilius Secundus in Novum Comum (Como, Northern Italy) around 61 AD. He was a lawyer, author of hundreds of letters of which 247 still survive to this day. He wrote to emperors and historians such as Tacitus and served as an imperial magistrate under Trajan. In one letter, Pliny requests Emperor Trajan's guidance regarding the Christians and their trials.

What we learn about Christians of the first century is their view of who Jesus is, "that they were accustomed to meet on a fixed day before dawn and sing responsively a hymn to Christ as to a god."[16] This is exactly what Saint Paul writes in his letter to the Philippians. Jesus is God incarnate.

> Who, though he was in the form of God, did not count equality with God a thing to be grasped, but emptied himself, by taking the form of a servant, being born in the likeness of men. And being found in human form, he humbled himself by becoming obedient to the point of death, even death on a cross. Therefore God has highly exalted him and bestowed on him the name that is above every name, so that at the name of Jesus every knee should bow, in heaven and on earth and under the earth, and every tongue confess that Jesus Christ is Lord, to the glory of God the Father. (Phil 2:6–11)

Christianity's creedal cry is that Jesus is God incarnate who died, was buried, and rose again from the dead for the forgiveness of all our sins. Christians do not follow Jesus as a good teacher, miracle worker (maybe), or revolutionary. Jesus is both God and man who died on the cross so that we may be brought back to God having our sins forgiven and new life given to us. We do not just admire Jesus. We worship him as God. Pliny's complaint to the emperor was that Christians called Jesus Lord and would not give that title to Trajan or any emperor before or after. From the earliest non-New Testament account we see that Christians believed Jesus to be God himself incarnate and Lord of all. Therefore, at the name of Jesus, knees buckle and bow either out of love and reverence or in judgment. This creed teaches us that Jesus is equally God and man and at the end, every tongue will make this confession: Jesus Christ is Lord.

---

16. Pliny the Younger, "Pliny the Younger and Trajan on Christians," para. 4.

The Preeminence of Christ

> He is the image of the invisible God, the firstborn of all creation. For by him all things were created, in heaven and on earth, visible and invisible, whether thrones or dominions or rulers or authorities—all things were created through him and for him. And he is before all things, and in him all things hold together. And he is the head of the body, the church. He is the beginning, the firstborn from the dead, that in everything he might be preeminent. For in him all the fullness of God was pleased to dwell, and through him to reconcile to himself all things, whether on earth or in heaven, making peace by the blood of his cross. Colossians 1:15-20

Here in this text the apostle Paul begins to introduce his reputation of the Colossian heresy which appears to be that Christ is not God. So what is being called into question is what is known as Christology in this understanding of who Jesus is, predates the apostle Paul. As seen especially in the apostle promises creedal confession, the Christian church knew and believed Jesus to be God and man. Earlier I wrote that Paul often quoted hymns. Here is another early Christian him which would be some, is Pliny the younger would complain later, "to Christ as to a God."[17]

Paul's use of the term image reflects the understanding that lost the image of God but in Christ, the second Adam, God's image is restored. The term "firstborn of all creation" has been misunderstood by many throughout church history. Arius, a fourth-century heretic, thought this meant that Jesus was part of creation. However, everywhere else in Scripture that term firstborn means "one who is privileged" (Exod 4:22). It is rightly understood that this term "firstborn" does not mean Jesus is part of creation but rather that he is the cause of creation. If we go back to the gospel of John it says "in the beginning was the Word, and the Word was with God, was God. He was in the beginning with God. All things were made through him and without him was not anything made that was made" (John 1:1–3). The resurrection is also prominent in this passage when Paul says "the firstborn from the dead." Here is the key point to all of Christianity: the resurrection of Jesus Christ. Again I reiterate, apart from the resurrection we are still in our sins as Saint Paul says. If we fail to emphasize this key doctrine of the Christian faith then we have not defended or proclaimed the only hope anyone has.

---

17. Pliny the Younger, "Pliny the Younger and Trajan on Christians," para. 4.

> Great indeed, we confess, is the mystery of godliness:
> He was manifested in the flesh,
> vindicated by the Spirit,
> seen by angels,
> proclaimed among the nations,
> believed on in the world,
> taken up in glory. (1 Tim 3:16)

We have this text from 1 Timothy, another early Christian creed. As I've noted previously, songs and poems are retained more effectively in our memory and in our hearts. In fact, Timothy calls this something that "we confess." It is a mystery but it is a mystery of godliness. It is not believed in the world but it must be proclaimed. For those who come to believe it is no longer a mystery because we understand that Jesus came in a flash, incarnate by the spirit, proven to be God through miracles, and seen by angels. This is what we proclaim all around the world to every tongue, tribe, and nation. We proclaim that Jesus is both God and man coequal, coeternal, and coexistent with God the Father and the Spirit.

I have often used this text when proclaiming and defending the faith with both Latter-day Saints (Mormons) and Jehovah's Witnesses. It is one of the most succinct creeds and confessions that we have in the New Testament. Since I am a strict believer in the truth that God says in his word that the gospel is the power of God unto salvation (Rom 1:16) then even when utilizing the Apostles' Creed, I will commit to memory these specific creeds in the Scriptures so that I can show them from God's word the truths that have been simplified in the Creed. I encourage you to review these biblical creeds, these "I believe" statements, so that you are better equipped to defend and proclaim the one true God.

> Follow the pattern of the sound words that you have heard from me, in the faith and love that are in Christ Jesus. (2 Tim 1:13)

What are these sound words? What is this pattern? I'm convinced that the apostle Paul is talking about the New Testament documents and later we could add in the Apostles' Creed and all these biblical statements. The above texts and the ones below this particular one are the "pattern of sound words" that we are to proclaim. There is no need to get fancy. There is certainly a warning against going down a rabbit hole with a skeptic. Therefore, utilizing the creeds in the Bible and the Apostles' Creed helps us to focus on the essentials. (I do realize I keep repeating this point but it is absolutely necessary for you to remember.)

> Remember: Jesus Christ, raised from the dead, the offspring of David, as preached in my gospel. (2 Tim 2:8)

In this text we find a very simple and short creedal statement. What does it tell us first? Paul tells us to keep this in mind. In other words, memorize it. Paul calls Jesus the Christ which references back to the apostle Peter's creedal confession "You are the Christ the son of the living God" (cf. Matt 16:16). So we remember that Jesus is both God and man and that he died, because you can't rise from the dead unless you've first died. So Jesus really did die and physically rise from the dead. Also let us remember that by saying "offspring of David" Paul is reminding us of all the prophetic promises given through the writers of the Old Testament. That Jesus fulfilled prophecies is key to our apologetic tactics.

> Beloved, although I was very eager to write to you about our common salvation, I found it necessary to write appealing to you to contend for the faith that was once for all delivered to the saints. (Jude 3)

Throughout this chapter I have endeavored to point out the creeds of the Bible. I have tried to explain them in a way that you can then apply to your defense and proclamation of the Christian faith to those who come in and ask you about it. In the collection of writings known as the Anti-Nicene fathers there is a quote from Polycarp regarding how we must make sure we are offering true teachings when we defend and proclaim the faith. It says, "Forsaking the vanity of many, and there false doctrines, let us return to the word which has been handed down to us from the beginning."[18] They were delivered to the saints and there is no new revelation from God as it is complete in Jesus Christ. I leave you with one final creedal treatment from the letter to the Hebrew Christians.

> Therefore, leaving the word concerning the beginning of Christ, let us go on to perfection (maturity), not playing again a foundation of repentance from dead works, and of faith in God, of the doctrine of baptism, and of laying on of hands, and of resurrection from the dead, and of eternal punishment. (Heb 6:1–2)

Look again at the key teachings:

---

18. Roberts and Donaldson, *Apostolic Fathers*, 34.

- Christ: back to that statement of faith by Peter to Jesus, "You are the Christ, the son of the living God"
- Repentance: that which is needed most to repent and believe
- Faith: not just any faith but faith in God who gave us his only begotten son to save us from our sins
- Baptism: as Peter so directly states in his letter, "Baptism now saves you"
- Laying on of hands: this became the practice especially for those receiving ordination
- Resurrection: what better proof do we have that everything Jesus taught us and did for us is true than that he physically rose from the dead, never to die, and that is what we hope for as well?
- Eternal punishment: first, that those who believe these things no longer need fear eternal punishment. Second, that those who do not know this or simply do not believe it when they are told the gospel will suffer eternal punishment.

The teachings found in the biblical creeds are the essentials we are to focus upon when engaging the unbeliever and skeptic. Traveling outside those bounds can lead to error, speculation, and detracts from the proper gospel presentation. The Apostles' Creed gives us these teachings in a simple and succinct manner which helps us stay on topic and bring them to the Door of salvation, Jesus Christ.

Dear reader, please never forget that those who are coming to you who are not in the Christian faith are in eternal danger. As one of my favorite missionaries, David Brainerd, once said, and I paraphrase here, they walk by us with the fires of hell licking at their heels. When we realize that they are people for whom Christ died, and need him most desperately, and that apart from believing and receiving him in faith through the word and sacraments, they are eternally lost, how can we not prepare a defense and give them a reason for the hope within us? How can we not tell them that in Jesus Christ there is forgiveness of sins and life everlasting? Who are we to hoard for ourselves the eternal treasures of God? Who are we to hold anything back? Scripture tells us we are to owe no one anything but love and what is the most loving thing we can do? Tell them about Jesus. After all, "How will they call on him in whom they have not believed? And how are they to believe in him of whom they have never heard? And how are they to hear without someone preaching (proclaiming)?" (cf. Rom 10:14–15). We have the message of true hope and the One who is the very word of eternal life.

As you proclaim and defend the Christian faith keep in mind that the pattern of creedal statements began in the Old Testament which has continued through the writings of the apostles. Since the earliest church fathers, those who came right after the apostles themselves continued this practice so that the church, scattered around the globe, would maintain fidelity to the true faith, should encourage us to remain faithful as well. Using the Apostles' Creed does just that: keeps us on point and in agreement with the Scriptures. May God grant you grace to both proclaim and defend our most holy faith.

CHAPTER 4

Ancient Creeds

The Apostles' Creed

I believe in God, the Father Almighty,
Maker of heaven and earth.
And in Jesus Christ, His only Son, our Lord,
who was conceived by the Holy Spirit, born of the Virgin Mary,
suffered under Pontius Pilate,
was crucified, died and was buried.
He descended into hell.
The third day He rose again from the dead.
He ascended into heaven and sits at the right hand
of God the Father Almighty.
From thence He will come to judge the living and the dead.
I believe in the Holy Spirit, the holy Christian Church,
the communion of saints,
the forgiveness of sins, the
resurrection of the body,
and the life everlasting. Amen.

WE NOW TURN OUR eyes to the early church and their creedal statements (also called "rule of faith"). As you will come to find, the early leaders from second-generation Christianity onward simply followed the pattern handed down to them. Similarly, they were also writing these statements for two reasons: to train and teach new converts about the essentials of the Christian faith and to defend the faith against error and heresies continuing to creep into the church. As you read each of these creeds ponder how they reiterated the creeds of the New Testament and the teachings of Scripture.

Unity of the Faith

I will begin this section on the early church and the many ancient creeds of Christianity because it shows a unity of faith which was summarized and based upon the teachings of the apostles found in the New Testament Scriptures. Here, amongst the next generation of Christians, we find unity in doctrine and faith. Unlike a popular view, that somehow the church became corrupt, we find these creedal statements echoing those in the New Testament written by the apostles themselves. Far from a departing of the one true faith once handed down, we find a fidelity to the teachings of Scripture. In fact, we find them writing and passing these down because some were departing from the faith and they were endeavoring to maintain orthodoxy as various heresies began to creep in. It does the modern Christian good to read these creeds and confess them too.

Many modern-day evangelicals have difficulty with creedal statements and will reject them out of hand. However, the church has never feared them and, as shown in the previous chapter, the prophets and apostles wrote many creeds in the Scriptures. These are the essentials of the Christian faith which must be believed in order to even call yourself a Christian. Vary from these key doctrines and your version of Christianity should be questioned. Stay on these points and you will present the orthodox and true Christian faith. J. N. D. Kelly, in his excellent work on the creeds, reminds us that the pattern became universal both to teach new converts as well as to defend the faith. He writes,

> Prior to the beginning of the fourth century all creeds and summaries of faith were local in character. It was taken for granted, of course, that they enshrined the universally accepted Catholic faith, handed down from the Apostles. But they owed their immediate authority, no less than their individual stamp, to the liturgy of the local church in which they had emerged. Moreover, while creed-like formularies were to be found in the Eucharist, in the rite of exorcism and elsewhere, those in the main line of development were confined to baptism and the catechetical preparation leading up to it.[1]

---

1. Kelly, *Early Christian Creeds*, 205.

Irenaeus's "Rule of Faith"

Saint Irenaeus of Lyons was a student of the Bishop Polycarp, a disciple of the apostle John (yes, *that* John) who was one of the Twelve Apostles of Jesus. Irenaeus was probably born about 135–40 AD and this creed was an apologetic response to those who rejected the Christian faith as well as heretics developing new doctrine within the church. He would become the church leader of Lugdunum in Gaul (now Lyon, France) and wrote extensively against Gnosticism, which the apostle John battled in his letters in the New Testament.

Irenaeus wrote about creeds in his work against the gnostics,

> As I have already observed, the Church, having received this preaching and this faith, although scattered throughout the whole world, yet, as if occupying but one house, carefully preserves it. She also believes these points [of doctrine] just as if she had but one soul, and one and the same heart, and she proclaims them, and teaches them, and hands them down, with perfect harmony, as if she possessed only one mouth. For, although the languages of the world are dissimilar, yet the import of the tradition is one and the same. For the Churches which have been planted in Germany do not believe or hand down anything different, nor do those in Spain, nor those in Gaul, nor those in the East, nor those in Egypt, nor those in Libya, nor those which have been established in the central regions of the world. But as the sun, that creature of God, is one and the same throughout the whole world, so also the preaching of the truth shineth everywhere, and enlightens all men that are willing to come to a knowledge of the truth. Nor will any one of the rulers in the Churches, however highly gifted he may be in point of eloquence, teach doctrines different from these (for no one is greater than the Master); nor, on the other hand, will he who is deficient in power of expression inflict injury on the tradition. For the faith being ever one and the same, neither does one who is able at great length to discourse regarding it, make any addition to it, nor does one, who can say but little diminish it.[2]

Note that Irenaeus states that they "received" the teachings and the faith just like the apostle Paul, which I showed above from his own letters, utilized that term. Then he tells how "she" (that would be the church) proclaims them, teaches them, and "hands them down". They were not individual statements of faith from congregation to congregation, as is

2. Irenaeus, "Chapter 10," 49.

the custom today from independent churches. Instead, they were the same doctrines, "as if she had but one soul, and one and the same heart . . . and possessed only one mouth." Here is the unity of faith so many clamor for and yet, because they want their individual statements of faith in their independent churches, they reject what God has already blessed the church with from of old.

Look at the churches Irenaeus lists as having this unified creedal teaching, this unity of faith and doctrine: Germany, Gaul, Spain, Egypt, Libya, and throughout the whole world. Though language and culture differed, their doctrines, the teachings, the creeds were identical "as if one soul . . . one heart . . . one mouth." Oh wouldn't it be wonderful if the church throughout our modern world could say this same thing: "We confess with one soul, one heart and one mouth."

These churches did not write and create independent statements of faith but held tightly to that which they had "received." In Irenaeus's account he testifies that he received them from Polycarp who was disciple by the apostle John. In Irenaeus's work *Against Heresies*, we find the "Rule of Faith" which is a simple creedal statement from the second century (ca. 160). He writes what the church believes:

> In one God, the Father Almighty,
>
> who made the heaven and the earth
>
> and the seas and all the things that are in them;
>
> And in one Christ Jesus, the Son of God, who was made flesh for our salvations;
>
> And in the Holy Spirit, who made known through the prophets the plan of salvation, and the coming, and the birth from a virgin,
>
> and the passion, and the resurrection from the dead, and the bodily ascension into heaven of the beloved Christ Jesus, our Lord,
>
> and his future appearing from heaven in the glory of the Father
>
> to sum up all things and to raise anew all flesh of the whole human race.[3]

At this point, you may be saying, "Well, that looks very much like the Apostles' Creed at the beginning of this chapter." The similarities are, for me, breathtaking. Here the early church, second century, is reiterating

---

3. Irenaeus, "Chapter 10," 48–49.

what we find in the Word of God in a simple and concise manner which can be memorized and shared when someone asks what we believe. They are not creating new doctrine but repeating that which was delivered to the churches found in the New Testament to those churches now springing up all throughout the world.

As I've studied the Bible and church history, I have found that throughout the ages, God has given his church wonderful and faithful men who have maintained fidelity to what his word teaches. When you go back to the middle of the first century and find these creeds are echoing those in the New Testament and then move to the second and third centuries and find them all over the world where the gospel had been preached, you have to realize that a great gift has been given that too many have rejected out of hand. When reading this statement from Irenaeus, is there anything you cannot say "Amen" to? Is there anything that goes against the creeds from the Old and New Testament that we went through in the previous chapter? Is there anything written in it that you cannot agree with? Then, why try to reinvent the wheel? Every time an independent church develops its own statement of belief that is what they're doing. Stop. Reread the Apostles' Creed and the others in this chapter (and also at the end of the book where I've placed them all for easy reference) and see the treasure we have. In these creeds we have what we need to both defend and proclaim the Christian faith.

Old Roman Symbol (Creed) ca. second century

> I believe in God the Father almighty;
> and in Christ Jesus His only Son, our Lord,
> Who was born of the Holy Spirit and the Virgin Mary,
> Who under Pontius Pilate was crucified and buried,
> on the third day rose again from the dead,
> ascended to heaven,
> sits at the right hand of the Father,
> whence He will come to judge the living and the dead;
> and in the Holy Spirit,
> the holy Church,
> the remission of sins,
> the resurrection of the flesh
> (the life everlasting).

Several years ago I came across this "Old Roman Symbol" or creed and was reminded of it again just recently. It doesn't surprise me that so many Christians today are unfamiliar with the "Old Roman Symbol." We live in a time when the distance between the early church and the contemporary church has actually contributed to Christians being mostly ignorant of the history of the shaping of the creeds and even the creeds themselves.

Soon after Pentecost, as discussed earlier, the apostles began to develop creedal statements. We've reviewed those in this book in the previous chapter and learned, or maybe had our memory refreshed, that even in the Old Testament there were creedal statements, and the "I Believe" statements of faith. We even have an example of a church council, the first one to be held in Jerusalem, where the apostles were dealing with the specifics that needed to be believed in order to be of the true faith. This process was simply followed as the church moved on from the resurrection and ascension of Jesus, the time of the apostles and into what is called the early church fathers.

As you read this old Roman creed you probably can't help but notice the similarities to the Apostles' Creed. Historically, this is viewed as an earlier and shorter version of the Apostles' Creed. The second-century church fathers Tertullian and Irenaeus mention this creed in their own writings. This appears to have been the basic essentials taught to those who would be catechized into the Christian faith.

The Interrogatory Creed of Hippolytus
(ca. 170–235 AD)

Hippolytus was an early church leader and in order to ensure that the young believers under his care had a correct understanding of God the Father, Jesus the Son and the Holy Spirit, developed these questions which they needed to learn prior to their baptism. These were adult converts, leaders of their homes, who would then bring their entire household to the font of baptism after their time of catechism. Hippolytus used these as instructional statements to ensure that they had a correct understanding of the Christian faith and it's essential doctrines.

"Do you believe in God, the Father Almighty?"

"Do you believe in Christ Jesus, the Son of God, who was born of the Virgin Mary, and was crucified under Pontius Pilate, and was dead and buried, and rose again the third day, alive from the dead, and ascended into heaven, and sat at the right hand of the Father, and will come to judge the living and the dead?"

"Do you believe in the Holy Spirit, in the holy church, and the resurrection of the body?"

As we continue to work our way through the early church fathers, take notice of all that is familiar in the Apostles' Creed with baptismal formulas and apologetic letters for the defense of the faith. The Creed has a foundation in the early church but even more in the Holy Scriptures. We believers have a wonderful tool which the ancient church deemed useful for the training of new believers in the essentials of the faith and used in its defense as well. Though we do not know exactly when the Apostles' Creed was written we can see that very early in the church the key doctrines contained in it were already being formulated into creedal statements.

Ignatius of Antioch (50–110 AD)

> On this account also they were persecuted, being inspired by His grace to fully convince the unbelieving that there is one God, who has manifested Himself by Jesus Christ His Son, who is His eternal Word, not proceeding forth from silence, and who in all things pleased Him that sent Him.[4]
>
> The Evangelists, too, when they declared that the one Father was "the only true God," did not omit what concerned our Lord, but wrote: "In the beginning was the Word, and the Word was with God, and the Word was God."[5]
>
> For if there is one God of the universe, the Father of Christ, "of whom are all things;" and one Lord Jesus Christ, our [Lord], "by whom are all things;" and also one Holy Spirit, who wrought in Moses, and in the prophets and apostles; and also one baptism, which is administered that we should have fellowship with the death of the Lord; and also one elect Church; there ought likewise to be but one faith in respect to Christ. For there is one Lord, one faith, one baptism; one God and Father of all, who is through all, and in all.[6]
>
> There is then one God and Father, and not two or three; One who is; and there is no other besides Him, the only true [God]. For

---

4. Ign. *Magn.* 8.
5. Ign. *Ant.* 4.
6. Ign. *Phil.* 1.

"the Lord thy God," saith [the Scripture], "is one Lord." And again, "Hath not one God created us? Have we not all one Father? And there is also one Son, God the Word. For "the only-begotten Son," saith [the Scripture], "who is in the bosom of the Father." And again, "One Lord Jesus Christ." And in another place, "What is His name, or what His Son's name, that we may know?" And there is also one Paraclete. For "there is also," saith [the Scripture], "one Spirit," since we have been called in one hope of our calling.[7]

Ignatius answered, "Thou art in error when thou callest the demons of the nations gods. For there is but one God, who made heaven, and earth, and the sea, and all that are in them; and one Jesus Christ, the only-begotten Son of God, whose kingdom may I enjoy."[8]

The Baptismal Creed of Jerusalem: The Mystagogy, Cyril of Jerusalem ca. 350 AD

(Known from fourth-century patriarch Cyril of Jerusalem's Catechetical Lectures)

I believe in one God, the Father Almighty, Maker of heaven and earth, and of all things visible and invisible;

And in one Lord Jesus Christ, the only begotten Son of God, begotten of the Father before the ages, true God, by whom all things were made, who was incarnate and made man, crucified and buried, and rose again on the third day, and ascended into the heavens, and sat down at the right hand of the Father, and is coming to judge quick and dead.

And in the Holy Ghost, the Paraclete, who spake by the prophets;

And in one holy catholic Church; and resurrection of the flesh; and in life everlasting.[9]

---

7. Ign. *Phil.* 2.
8. Ign. *Martyr.* 2.
9. Roberts and Donaldson, *Apostolic Fathers*, 31.

Clement of Rome (50–97 AD)

Why are there strifes, and tumults, and divisions, and schisms, and wars among you? Have we not [all] one God and one Christ? Is there not one Spirit of grace poured out upon us?[10]

We beseech Thee, Lord and Master, to be our help and succor. Save those among us who are in tribulation; have mercy on the lowly; lift up the fallen; show Thyself unto the needy; heal the ungodly; convert the wanderers of Thy people; feed the hungry; release our prisoners; raise up the weak; comfort the fainthearted. Let all the Gentiles know that Thou art the God alone, and Jesus Christ is Thy Son, and we are Thy people and the sheep of Thy pasture.[11]

For concerning faith and repentance and genuine love and temperance and sobriety and patience we have handled every argument, putting you in remembrance, that ye ought to please Almighty God in righteousness and truth and long suffering with holiness, laying aside malice and pursuing concord in love and peace, being instant in gentleness; even as our fathers, of whom we spake before, pleased Him, being lowly minded toward their Father and God and Creator and towards all men.[12]

---

10. 1 Clem. 46.
11. 1 Clem. 59.
12. 1 Clem. 62.

Polycarp of Smyrna (69–155 AD)

Jesus is Lord.

This was the creedal statement of Polycarp the Bishop of Smyrna. Upon his arrest, trial and execution, it was demanded of Polycarp to renounce Jesus Christ and call Caesar Lord. This short creedal statement would result in the death of many Christians over the early centuries of the church. Polycarp refused, allegedly saying, "Bring them on, then, for we are not accustomed to repent of what is good in order to adopt that which is evil." This was his response to the proconsul's threat to have the beasts released to tear him apart in the arena as thousands called for his death. These three short words encapsulate the core teaching of Christianity: Jesus is Lord, Master, God, and there is none other. During the early years of Christianity to say this was to sign your own death warrant. While many today may say it, how many would confess this as they faced martyrdom?

We have, within the text of his letter to the Philippians, further evidence of the creedal formulations given by the apostles to their own disciples (Polycarp was a disciple of the apostle John). Here, Polycarp writes,

> The strong root of your faith, spoken of in days long passed, have lasted until now and borne fruit to our Lord Jesus Christ, who suffered even to the point of death for our sins, but whom God raised from the dead, releasing the grip of Hades. "He is the one that though you do not see, you believe in, and, believing, you rejoice with joy unspeakable and full of glory" (1 Pet. 1:8). Into this joy many long to enter, knowing that "by grace you are saved, not of works, but by the will of God through Jesus Christ" (Eph. 2:8-9 w. Jn. 1:13).[13]

Note well the points of doctrine in his very first chapter and throughout as noted:

Jesus is Lord (when Polycarp refers to him as Christ)—also found in chapter 2

Suffered—also in chapter 4 and 8

Died—also in chapter 8

Raised from the dead—also in chapter 8 and 9

Ascended (though you do not see, you believe)

---

13. Pol. *Phil.* 1.

Once again we see the essentials of the Christian faith marked out in a succinct manner. Consider the continuation of this teaching throughout the epistle when Polycarp says,

> Therefore, prepare yourselves for the race and serve the Lord in fear and truth like people who have forsaken the useless, empty talk and the errors of the multitude and believed in the One who raised up our Lord Jesus Christ from the dead and gave him glory and a throne at his right hand.
>
> All things in heaven and on earth are subject to him. Every spirit serves him. He comes as the Judge of the living and the dead. God will require justice for his blood from those who do not believe in Him.
>
> But the One who raised Christ from the dead will raise us also, if we do his will, walk in his commandments, love what he loved, and keep ourselves from all unrighteousness, greed, love of money, evil speaking, and lies.[14]

The epistle continues with instructions to teach the doctrines to their wives, children, and those new in the faith. He also writes of the importance of remaining faithful to the doctrines passed down to them when he says, "Let us return to the message which has been handed down to us from the beginning."[15] Polycarp, himself a disciple of an Apostle, quotes much of Paul and the others and encourages the believers to say with the truth delivered to them instead of the gnostic heresies infiltrating the Church.

The following quotes (italics as emphasis of doctrine) will hopefully enable you to see that these creedal statements are passed down from generation to generation. Looking at the dates included next to the Ancient Church Fathers Names, is given so that you can see they were not too far in years from the Apostles themselves and many learned these things as they were passed down the generation(s).

Irenaeus of Lyons (115–202 AD)

> And others of them, with great craftiness, adapted such parts of Scripture to their own figments, lead away captive from the truth those who do not retain a steadfast faith in one God, the Father Almighty, and in one Lord Jesus Christ, the Son of God. Against Heresies, Book I. Chapter III. 6.

14. Pol. *Phil.* 2.
15. Pol. *Phil.* 7.

> The fallacy, then, of this exposition is manifest. For when John, proclaiming one God, the Almighty, and one Jesus Christ, the Only-begotten, by whom all things were made, declares that this was the Son of God, this the Only-begotten, this the Former of all things, this the true Light who enlighteneth every man, this the Creator of the world, this He that came to His own, this He that became flesh and dwelt among us,–these men, by a plausible kind of exposition, perverting these statements, maintain that there was another Monogenes, according to production, whom they also style Arche. Against Heresies, Book I. Chapter IX. 2.
>
> But if the Word of the Father who descended is the same also that ascended, He, namely, the Only-begotten Son of the only God, who, according to the good pleasure of the Father, became flesh for the sake of men, the apostle certainly does not speak regarding any other, or concerning any Ogdoad, but respecting our Lord Jesus Christ. Against Heresies, Book I. Chapter IX. 3.
>
> The Church, though dispersed through our the whole world, even to the ends of the earth, has received from the apostles and their disciples this faith: [She believes] in one God, the Father Almighty, Maker of heaven, and earth, and the sea, and all things that are in them; and in one Christ Jesus, the Son of God, who became incarnate for our salvation; and in the Holy Spirit, who proclaimed through the prophets the dispensations of God.[16]

I pause here to interject some thoughts on what is being taught. First, this is what the church received from the apostles and their disciples of the Christian faith. This is not new teaching but reiterates the essentials of the faith. Second, when Irenaeus says "she believes" he is speaking of the church worldwide, the bride of Christ. This is the faith universal. Therefore, what is believed among the early Christians? Let me write each statement separate and notice, once again, how similar it is to the formula we have in the Apostles' Creed.

> One God
>
> Father Almighty
>
> Make of heaven and earth, the sea and all things
>
> One Jesus Christ
>
> Son of God
>
> Incarnate

---

16. Irenaeus, *Haer.* 1.10.1.

For our salvation

The Holy Spirit

Who proclaimed through the prophets what would come to pass (dispensations of God)

This is quite remarkable and perhaps new information to many in the modern evangelical world. While these are the writings of men, Irenaeus reminds his readers that they were directly received from the apostles. Review the chapter before on the New Testament creeds and I would challenge you to find anything different between them and this statement of faith and creed.

> The rule of truth which we hold is that there is one God Almighty, who made all things by His Word, and fashioned and formed, out of that which had no existence, all things which exist. Thus saith the Scripture, to that effect: "By the Word of the Lord were the heavens established, and all the might of them, by the spirit of His mouth." And again, "All things were made by Him, and without Him was nothing made."[17]

When Irenaeus wrote his book *Against Heresies* he was dealing with those who were rejecting the faith delivered to the Church by the Apostles. This "Rule of Faith" is so similar in content to the Apostles' Creed that many believe it is the foundation for it.[18]

Once again, note what is taught:

One God Almighty

Creator

By His Word (Jesus, cf. John 1:1)

This is the first part, as Luther divides it, of the Apostles' Creed. Over and over, in each of the books from his *Against Heresies*, Irenaeus reiterates that God is our Father, the Almighty, and Creator of all things. In many sections he states that all things were created through the word, pointing to Jesus of whom the apostle John says is the word through which all things were made, and as Saint Paul says, all things are sustained (cf. Col 1:15–20)

> It is proper, then, that I should begin with the first and most important head, that is, God the Creator, who made the heaven

17. Irenaeus, *Haer.* 1.22.1.
18. Schaff, "Name and Definition," 4.

and the earth, and all things that are therein (whom these men blasphemously style the fruit of a defect), and to demonstrate that there is nothing either above Him or after Him; nor that, influenced by any one, but of His own free will, He created all things, since He is the only God, the only Lord, the only Creator, the only Father, alone containing all things, and Himself commanding all things into existence.[19]

Now, that this God is the Father of our Lord Jesus Christ, Paul the apostle also has declared, [saying,] "There is one God, the Father, who is above all, and through all things, and in us all." I have indeed proved already that there is only one God; but I shall further demonstrate this from the apostles themselves, and from the discourses of the Lord. For what sort of conduct would it be, were we to forsake the utterances of the prophets, of the Lord, and of the apostles, that we might give heed to these persons, who speak not a word of sense?[20]

That God is the Creator of the world is accepted even by those very persons who in many ways speak against Him, and yet acknowledge Him, styling Him the Creator, and an angel, not to mention that all the Scriptures call out [to the same effect], and the Lord teaches us of this Father who is in heaven, and no other, as I shall show in the sequel of this work. For the present, however, that proof which is derived from those who allege doctrines opposite to ours, is of itself sufficient,–all men, in fact, consenting to this truth: the ancients on their part preserving with special care, from the tradition of the first-formed man, this persuasion, while they celebrate the praises of one God, the Maker of heaven and earth; others, again, after them, being reminded of this fact by the prophets of God, while the very heathen learned it from creation itself. For even creation reveals Him who formed it, and the very work made suggests Him who made it, and the world manifests Him who ordered it. The Universal Church, moreover, through the whole world, has received this tradition from the apostles.[21]

But there is one only God, the Creator—He who is above every Principality, and Power, and Dominion, and Virtue: He is Father, He is God, He the Founder, He the Maker, He the Creator, who made those things by Himself, that is, through His Word and His Wisdom— heaven and earth, and the seas, and all things that are in them: He is just; He is good; He it is who formed man, who

---

19. Irenaeus, *Haer.* 2.1.1.
20. Irenaeus, *Haer.* 2.2.5.
21. Irenaeus, *Haer.* 2.9.1.

planted paradise, who made the world, who gave rise to the flood, who saved Noah; He is the God of Abraham, and the God of Isaac, and the God of Jacob, the God of the living: He it is whom the law proclaims, whom the prophets preach, whom Christ reveals, whom the apostles make known to us, and in whom the Church believes. He is the Father of our Lord Jesus Christ: through His Word, who is His Son, through Him He is revealed and manifested to all to whom He is revealed; for those [only] know Him to whom the Son has revealed Him. But the Son, eternally coexisting with the Father, from of old, yea, from the beginning, always reveals the Father to Angels, Archangels, Powers, Virtues, and all to whom He wills that God should be revealed.[22]

Now, that the preaching of the apostles, the authoritative teaching of the Lord, the announcements of the prophets, the dictated utterances of the apostles, and the ministration of the law–all of which praise one and the same Being, the God and Father of all, and not many diverse beings, nor one deriving his substance from different gods or powers, but [declare] that all things [were formed] by one and the same Father (who nevertheless adapts [His works] to the natures and tendencies of the materials dealt with), things visible and invisible, and, in short, all things that have been made [were created] neither by angels, nor by any other power, but by God alone, the Father–are all in harmony with our statements, has, I think, been sufficiently proved, while by these weighty arguments it has been shown that there is but one God, the Maker of all things.[23]

To which course many nations of those barbarians who believe in Christ do assent, having salvation written in their hearts by the Spirit, without paper or ink, and, *carefully preserving the ancient tradition, believing in one God, the Creator of heaven and earth, and all things therein, by means of Christ Jesus, the Son of God; who, because of His surpassing love towards His creation, condescended to be born of the virgin, He Himself uniting man through Himself to God, and having suffered under Pontius Pilate, and rising again, and having been received up in splendor, shall come in glory, the Savior of those who are saved, and the Judge of those who are judged, and sending into eternal fire those who transform the truth, and despise His Father and His advent.*[24]

---

22. Irenaeus, *Haer.* 2.30.9.
23. Irenaeus, *Haer.* 2.35.4.
24. Irenaeus, *Haer.* 3.4.2.

I have italicized the statement above to emphasize the creedal statement that was "carefully" preserved and handed down from the Apostles to the Churches throughout the world. These are the statements of faith that we are to hold fast to. These are the statements, derived from God's Holy Word, which though condensed into simpler form, are nevertheless what is to be confessed and believed.

> Thus then there is shown forth One God, the Father, not made, invisible, creator of all things; above whom there is no other God, and after whom there is no other God. And, since God is rational, therefore by (the) Word He created the things that were made; and God is Spirit, and by (the) Spirit He adorned all things.[25]

> This then is the order of the *rule of our faith*, and the foundation of the building, and the stability of our conversation:
>
> God, the Father, not made, not material, invisible;
>
> one God, the creator of all things: this is *the first point of our faith*.
>
> The second point is:
>
> The Word of God, Son of God, Christ Jesus our Lord,
>
> who was manifested to the prophets according to the form of their prophesying and according to the method of the dispensation of the Father:
>
> through whom all things were made;
>
> who also at the end of the times, to complete and gather up all things,
>
> was made man among men, visible and tangible, in order to abolish death and show forth life and produce a community of union between God and man.
>
> And the third point is:
>
> The Holy Spirit, through whom the prophets prophesied,
>
> and the fathers learned the things of God,
>
> and the righteous were led forth into the way of righteousness;
>
> and who in the end of the times was poured out in a new way
>
> upon mankind in all the earth, renewing man unto God.[26]

---

25. Irenaeus, *Epid.* 5.
26. Irenaeus, *Epid.* 6.

CREEDAL APOLOGETICS

As we begin to look specifically at the Apostles' Creed in the next chapter, keep in mind how Irenaeus's Rule of Faith is divided into three sections: Father, Son, and Holy Spirit. This division is what Martin Luther brought out in his Larger Catechism and the explanations. The trifold aspect of the Creed enables us to better focus upon what will be needed in our discussions with those outside the true faith.

Below are further quotes from the ancient church who continued the practice of handing down through each generation the essentials of the Christian faith. I quote them here so that you will see their own words and confessions which helped to later formulate the Apostles' Creed. Once again, I challenge those reading who may not appreciate the rich treasure given to the early church, to find any of these statements not in agreement with the holy word of God.

Theophilus of Antioch (120–90 AD)

> But God at least, the Father and Creator of the universe, did not abandon mankind, but gave a law, and sent holy prophets to declare and teach the race of men, that each one of us might awake and understand that there is one God.[27]

Athenagoras of Athen (133–90 AD)

> But, since our doctrine acknowledges one God, the Maker of this universe, who is Himself uncreated (for that which is does not come to be, but that which is not) but has made all things by the Logos which is from Him, we are treated unreasonably in both respects, in that we are both defamed and persecuted.[28]
>
> That we are not atheists, therefore, seeing that we acknowledge one God, uncreated, eternal, invisible, impassible, incomprehensible, illimitable, who is apprehended by the understanding only and the reason, who is encompassed by light, and beauty, and spirit, and power ineffable, by whom the universe has been created through His Logos, and set in order, and is kept in being—I have sufficiently demonstrated. [I say "His Logos"], for we acknowledge also a Son of God.[29]

27. Theophilus, *Autol.* 2.34.
28. Athenagoras, *Leg.* 4.
29. Athenagoras, *Leg.* 10.

Clement of Alexandria (155–215 AD)

"Now the just shall live by faith," which is according to the covenant and the commandments; since these, which are two in name and time, given in accordance with the [divine] economy—being in power one—the old and the new, are dispensed through the Son by one God.[30]

Wherefore also the apostle designates as "the express image [χαρακτῆρα] of the glory of the Father" the Son, who taught the truth respecting God, and expressed the fact that the Almighty is the one and only God and Father, "whom no man knoweth but the Son, and he to whom the Son shall reveal Him. That God is one is intimated by those "who seek the face of the God of Jacob;" whom being the only God, our Savior and God characterizes as the Good Father.[31]

Tertullian of Carthage (160–225 AD)

We, however, as we indeed always have done (and more especially since we have been better instructed by the Paraclete, who leads men indeed into all truth), believe that there is one only God, but under the following dispensation, or οἰκονομία, as it is called, *that this one only God has also a Son, His Word, who proceeded from Himself, by whom all things were made, and without whom nothing was made. Him we believe to have been sent by the Father into the Virgin, and to have been born of her—being both Man and God, the Son of Man and the Son of God, and to have been called by the name of Jesus Christ; we believe Him to have suffered, died, and been buried, according to the Scriptures, and, after He had been raised again by the Father and taken back to heaven, to be sitting at the right hand of the Father, and that He will come to judge the quick and the dead; who sent also from heaven from the Father, according to His own promise, the Holy Ghost, the Paraclete, the sanctifier of the faith of those who believe in the Father, and in the Son, and in the Holy Ghost.*[32]

---

30. Clement of Alexandria, *Strom.* 2.6.
31. Clement of Alexandria, *Strom.* 7.10.
32. Tertullian, *Prax.* 2.

Hippolytus of Rome (170–235 AD)

For it is right, in the first place, to expound the truth that the Father is one God, "of whom is every family," "by whom are all things, of whom are all things, and we in Him."[33]

If, therefore, all things are put under Him with the exception of Him who put them under Him, He is Lord of all, and the Father is Lord of Him, that in all there might be manifested one God, to whom all things are made subject together with Christ, to whom the Father hath made all things subject, with the exception of Himself. And this, indeed, is said by Christ Himself, as when in the Gospel He confessed Him to be His Father and His God. For He speaks thus: "I go to my Father and your Father, and to my God and your God."[34]

Gregory Thaumaturgus (213–70 AD)

There is one God, the Father of the living Word, who is His subsistent Wisdom and Power and Eternal Image: perfect Begetter of the perfect Begotten, Father of the only-begotten Son.[35]

Apostolic Constitutions

But we, who are the children of God and the sons of peace, do preach the holy and right word of piety, and declare one only God, the Lord of the law and of the prophets, the Maker of the world, the Father of Christ; not a being that caused Himself, or begat Himself, as they suppose, but eternal, and without original, and inhabiting light inaccessible; not two or three, or manifold, but eternally one only; not a being that cannot be known or spoken of, but who was preached by the law and the prophets; the Almighty, the Supreme Governor of all things, the All-powerful Being; the God and Father of the Only-begotten, and of the First-born of the whole creation; one God, the Father of one Son.[36]

Within this text we also have a prayer for catechumens (those adults new in the faith who have been taught in the essentials of the faith):

33. Hippolytus of Rome, *Haer.* 3.
34. Hippolytus of Rome, *Haer.* 6.
35. Gregory Thaumaturgus, "A Declaration of Faith."
36. "Apostolic Constitutions," 6.3.

ANCIENT CREEDS

> O God Almighty, unbegotten and inaccessible, who only art the true God, the God and Father of Your Christ, Your only begotten Son; the God of the Comforter, and Lord of the whole world; who by Christ appointed Your disciples to be teachers for the teaching of piety.[37]

Note how it reflects that which has been passed down from generation to generation from the apostles through the early church and now given to them. Included in this prayer are the teachings that God is our Father, Almighty. Jesus is the only begotten Son of God and the Holy Spirit is the Comforter (cf. John 17). It also speaks of Christ appointing the apostles to teach us these things which have been, as Saint Paul says, "delivered to us" (cf. 1 Cor. 15). Throughout this document, in its various prayers, we find similar creedal statements.

All of the quotes in this chapter are given to you so that you may see that creedal statements should not be disregarded or hidden away from. In fact, they should be more eagerly embraced because they are taken from the word of God and the teachings of the apostles. The Apostles' Creed is a simple way to state what Christians believe. While it is not an exhaustive theological work on all the doctrines of the faith (see the Nicene and Athanasian Creeds) it is the basics of the Christian Faith in a short manner conducive to memorization.

When engaging in apologetics the conversation can begin to focus on opinions of both the skeptic and believer. However, since the goal of apologetics is to bring them the gospel of Jesus Christ, his death, burial, and resurrection for the forgiveness of sins, the Apostles' Creed's brevity keeps us on track. So often, in my own discussions and debates with skeptics ended up down some rabbit hole and the conversation's point (Jesus died for the forgiveness of their sins) ends up being lost. As you can see from all these examples, and they are not all that are out there, the early church believed these truths to have been passed down to them from the apostles, their disciples and others living close to the apostolic days. These are those doctrines which we will now look into and begin to apply to general questions from skeptics when they ask us, "Why do you believe this is true?"

---

37. "Apostolic Constitutions," 2.6..

Apostles' Creed Part 1

I believe in God, the Father Almighty,

Maker of heaven and earth.

CHAPTER 5

I Believe in God the Father

"I believe" is where this Creed begins. Simply stated, it is what this statement is all about: the doctrines we hold to be absolutely true. However, what does "believe" actually mean? Why does the Apostles' Creed begin with these two words "believe"? What is actually held as objectively true?

In the Lutheran Church I attend, we often sing the Creed via this hymn:

> 1 We all believe in one true God,
> Father, Son, and Holy Ghost,
> Ever-present help in need,
> Praised by all the heav'nly host;
> All He made His love enfolds,
> All creation He upholds.
> 2 We all believe in Jesus Christ,
> Son of God and Mary's son,
> Who descended from His throne
> And for us salvation won;
> By whose cross and death are we
> Rescued from all misery.
> 3 We all confess the Holy Ghost,
> Who from both in truth proceeds,
> Who sustains and comforts us
> In all trials, fears, and needs.
> Blessed, holy Trinity,
> Praise forever be to Thee![1]

1. Lutheran Church—Missouri Synod, *Lutheran Service Book*, 953.

This hymn states clearly, in a metrical and musical manner, the essentials of the faith. In fact, this was the first hymn I memorized from the *Lutheran Service Book* and realized I was getting the Creed into my mind and heart as well. The link to this hymn is on my website at www.lutherangirl.org and in the appendix of this book.

As a reminder, the Apostles' Creed, arising from earlier creeds distills the message of the Gospel by answering the following:

- Who is this God?
- What has he done?
- Who is Jesus?
- Who is the Holy Spirit?

Furthermore, the structure of this creed is Trinitarian and focuses upon the person and work of Jesus Christ. The short narrative statements help us to remember the essentials of the faith as we answer questions posed to us. Also it defends the faith against distortion and misreading of Scripture or even misrepresentations of the gospel.[2] Churches throughout have found it necessary to defend the faith both within the church, from error and from without by skeptics and unbelievers alike.

Justo González, in *The Apostles' Creed for Today*, tries to break down the various ways of defining the "I believe." His book gives different levels of belief, some that are uncertain, some which offer an opinion which they are not willing to support, and then the introduction of "I believe" in a sentence which means I am fully confident in what's going to come after that statement.[3] The "I believe" of the Apostles' Creed is that final statement: I am fully confident what I am about to say. This does not mean that I am confident in my faith as a personal believing but instead in the faith which I am confessing.

When Christians begin the Apostles' Creed with "I believe in..." it is a confession that spans time. We are confessing what the church has believed from the beginning. We are not saying anything new or radical or independent of the church. In fact, as I have laid out in the previous chapters we are confessing boldly the essentials of the faith, with nothing based upon our opinion. We can change the very first word from the singular "I" to the plural "we." Karl Barth said it this way:

2. Wengert, *Dictionary of Luther and the Lutheran Traditions*, 129.
3. González, *Apostles' Creed for Today*.

> This "I believe" is consummated in a meeting with one who is not man but God, the father, son, and Holy Spirit, and by my believing I see myself completely filled and determines by this object of my faith . . . what interests me is not my faith, but he in whom "I Believe."[4]

Over the next few chapters we are going to be looking at specific statements within this creed and how it begins to apply to our apologetic discussions with unbelievers and skeptics alike. You may also find that you will be able to approach other Christians and help guide them in what is to be confessed and believed in order to be considered a true Christian. The primary focus of this book is the apologetic method which I have called "Creedal Apologetics." Therefore, as you go through these next few chapters it is my hope that you will find them very practical as well as informative. Looking at each of the three parts, as Martin Luther divided them, you will be able to defend the faith to those who are atheists straight through to those who may be Zoroastrians.

It is human to look to something or someone to cling to. We live in an age of uncertainty and one which says truth is subjective and relative to the person or situation. In life we experience events or people that test our trust and so it is that people look to another for solid footing. The atheist places it in his scientific knowledge. The spiritual and not-so-religious place it in contemporary styles. Some create a personal religion gathering from a wide mix of beliefs from the world. Many today have never even visited a church building nor do they know who Jesus is or anything about Christianity. The latter are amongst my own neighbors and so they wander through life without truth, objective truth.

When I began studying apologetics I often would become frustrated with the focus of the professor. It seemed to me that they were filled with giving me details about certain arguments from various apologetics styles and just never got to the application point where the rubber hits the road. Throughout this book I will be interspersing actual encounters I have had with children, adults, atheists, those of other religious persuasions, as well as the modern concept of "I'm not religious I'm just spiritual" type of people. How do you as a Christian utilize creedal apologetics in these discussions?

In the Apostles' Creed we have objective truth to be trusted, place our faith in and believe. However, it is not the what of something that we are proclaiming or confessing but the Who, the One Who is Truth. Jesus said

---

4. Barth, *Dogmatics in Outline*, 16.

he is the way, the truth, and the life and no one comes to the Father except through him. The Creed begins with him and not us. Dr. Montgomery is correct when he taught us that apologetics is not about our testimony but his and not what denominational peculiarities we prefer but what is to be a creedal defense of the Christian faith founded on facts.[5]

In chapter 2 I began with a subheading of "how do you know it's true". When the Apostles' Creed begins with the phrase "I believe" it is not talking about opinion. It is not talking about subjective feelings. It is speaking of the objective truths for which there is ample evidence. Simon Greenleaf wrote "The foundation of our religion is a basis of fact-the fact of the birth, ministry, miracles, death, resurrection by the evangelists as having actually occurred, within their own personal knowledge."[6] What Greenleaf is saying is that all the evidence we have for the Christian faith, based upon the teachings of the four Gospels, the evangelists' testimony in the book of Acts and their letters, as well as Moses and the prophets are factual and objective.

We do not use the term "I believe" as opinion but as objective truth. I cannot emphasize this enough in a postmodern world where truth is subjective. Try that subjectivism on any building project and it will soon fall apart. In the same way apply subjective arguments to the Christian faith and you have nothing other than the same thing as every other religion, a false faith. It was imperative in this book to begin with the biblical testimony, moving on to the apostolic testimony, through the early church testimony so that you the reader would understand this creed is based on the Bible and therefore, you may be comfortable utilizing it in your defense of the Christian faith.

Objective truths are what we are going to look at in each section of the Apostles' Creed. Just as Martin Luther divided it into three parts, so will our study in the following chapters. We will begin with the Father followed with the ministry and works of God the Son and finally the continued ministry in the church by God the Holy Spirit. This is definitely a Trinitarian structured creed.

---

5. This information came from in-person classes I took at the University of Strasbourg.
6. Greenleaf, "Testimony of the Evangelists by Simon Greenleaf," para. 3.

God as Father

To begin this section, we have to realize that the Creed describes what Christians believe quite briefly. It does not go into details on the Father, Son, and Holy Spirit but remains on what is essential to salvation for those outside of the Christian faith. It guides us in defending the faith and proclaiming the gospel by its very simplicity and succinctness. This Creed teaches us to know God fully as Father, Son, and Holy Spirit. In Martin Luther's Large Catechism, the notes say, "Since God is the maker of heaven and earth we realize that all we are all we will ever become, and so we possess depends entirely on our Creator."[7] This opening statement of the Creed teaches us about our absolute dependence on God and who he is as Father and Creator.

In Luther's Small Catechism, we have a beautiful and short explanation for this first article. Luther attributes this section to "Creation," asking the question "What does this mean?" His answer is so comforting that I want to begin our look at this section with it.

> I believe that God has made me and all creatures. He has given me my body and soul, eyes, ears, and all my limbs, my reason, and all my senses, and still preserves them. In addition, He has given me clothing and shoes, meat and drink, house and home, wife and children, fields, cattle, and all my goods. He provides me richly and daily with all that I need to support this body and life. He protects me from all danger and guards me and preserves me from all evil. He does this out of pure, fatherly, divine goodness and mercy, without any merit or worthiness in me. For all this I ought to thank Him, praise Him, serve Him and obey Him. This is most certainly true.[8]

I love Luther's Small Catechism on this the first article on creation when he writes, "What does this mean? Answer: I believe that God has made me and all creatures.[9]" This means he is the creator. This world did not just happen by accident or chance. The atheist will come to you and say, "How do you know there is a God?" How do we using the Apostles' Creed respond? We respond by saying, "Because God is my Father." As Father he created the heavens and the earth. The prophet Isaiah says, "[Who has] forgotten the

---

7. Dau, *Concordia*, 328.
8. Dau, *Concordia*, 328.
9. Dau, *Concordia*, 328.

Lord, your Maker, who stretched out the heavens and laid the foundations of the earth?" (Isa 51:13). The psalmist writes, "Oh come, let us worship and bow down; let us kneel before the Lord, our Maker!" (Ps 95:6).

At this point you may be saying to me, "Why aren't you telling me specific scientific answers?" The reason is because the gospel is the power of God unto salvation and not scientific reason, though often we find it proves God's word to be true. The word of God is that he has chosen to create and sustain true faith and not arguments over evolution or quantum physics. If we want to know who the Father is, this is how Jesus answered Philip when he came to him and said,

> "Lord, show us the Father, and it is enough for us." Jesus said to him, "Have I been with you so long, and you still do not know me, Philip? Whoever has seen me has seen the Father." (John 14:8–9)

If we want to see the heavenly father we must look to Jesus. The Creed says "I believe" in God the Father Almighty. This speaks of God's authority, power, and care. Everything we see was created by God, Paul says to the Christians in Rome, "For his invisible attributes, namely, his eternal power and divine nature, have been clearly perceived, ever since the creation of the world,[a] in the things that have been made. So they are without excuse" (Rom 1:20). However there is a limit of what we can know by the things he has seen which is why we need to point the skeptic and atheist to Jesus of Nazareth.

When we say God is Creator of heaven and earth we don't mean that the deist's God simply created it and left it to itself. When we Christians say God is our father we are speaking of that relationship which we have through Jesus Christ. We are also saying he still cares for us. As Martin Luther says in his answer to this statement in the first article his care is shown in the following ways:

> He has given me my body and soul, eyes, ears, and all my limbs, my reason, and all my senses, still preserves them. He continues by reminding us that God richly provides us daily what we need and protects us . . . He does this out of pure, fatherly, divine goodness and mercy, without any merit or worthiness in us.[10]

The One True God, whom we call God the Father in this Creed, is sustaining earth at the proper distance from the sun, keeping gravity in place, and keeping the atmosphere perfectly created for life to survive and

---

10. Dau, *Concordia*, 400.

keeps us. We call him Father because we believe in his Son, Jesus Christ, and have been adopted into his family. This is who we are to present to the unbeliever in our discussions.

However, you may be speaking with a person who did not have a good father figure in their life. Maybe there dad was missing. Maybe they don't even know who their father was. However, that does not negate the truth of God as our father who lovingly gives us all that we need and for that, Luther would say, I ought to thank him, praise him, serve him, and obey him. Once again the emphasis in our apologetic should be Jesus Christ because it is through him that we see the love and care of God as Father. God doesn't withhold anything from us and gives us more than we need for certainly deserve. It's here that we see the greatest way God cares for us in that he has given his only begotten son Jesus Christ who died, was buried, and rose again for the forgiveness of our sins.

Almighty Maker of Heaven and Earth

If we begin to wonder into the specifics of creation we end up in speculative discussions. Science does not know enough about the world to make a definitive statement that this all happened by chance. Ample evidence is building towards an understanding that this just couldn't happen by accident. There is enough scientific proof that a creator and designer is behind our universe. As Michael Behe, a microbiologist, has said in his book *Darwin's Black Box*, when you find certain proteins can only be created by those specific proteins which do not exist prior to those proteins forming you begin to see that creation is much more complicated and science does not have the answers for these things.[11]

So who is God as our Father? In a recent conversation with the neighbor about Jesus's death on a cross, the conversation then turned to God as our Father. He then said to me, "So I would have two fathers?" "Yes," I responded, "if you believe that Jesus died was buried and rose again for the forgiveness of your sins you would have two fathers. You would have your earthly father and a Heavenly Father." The conversation continued into what our Heavenly Father does for us. In comparing God the Father to his earthly father we began to discuss how his dad only does what is good for him and how he would never want to harm him. We discussed how much his earthly dad loves him. I then shared how God the Father loves him even

---

11. Behe, *Darwin's Black Box*, 20.

more than his earthly dad and how his care for him goes beyond anything his earthly dad can do. It was at that point that I said, "God the Father showed how much he loved you by sending his only son, Jesus Christ, to this world as a little baby who grew up understanding that we need to eat and drink, got tired, cried when his friend died, and went to the cross to be killed so that you might have eternal life." The young man was amazed that God would give up his son to die for us.

This is how you use the Apostles' Creed in talking about God the Father Almighty. When we are engaged in apologetics the point is to bring them the gospel. Yes, they will have specific questions regarding how this world came to be. How do I know there's a God? How do you know what you believe is true? The skill you must learn is to keep the conversation off of things you don't know and on that which you know is objectively true. Speculations on quantum physics and microbiology are subjects that are probably beyond our comprehension. In fact, most scientists understand that their speculations are just that, guesswork. There is no proof for the theories of evolution or quantum physics and therefore you should redirect the conversation off of those topics and on to what is necessary for salvation as quickly as you can. You are not dodging their questions but focusing on their greatest need: the forgiveness of sins.

The reason I keep saying that we need to continue to focus on the gospel is because that is the unbeliever's greatest need. Luther says this in great summary, "we find God's gracious fatherly heart only through the son; only the Holy Spirit leads us to the son." Jesus is the only One who shows us God the Father. God the Father shows us how much He loves us in the gifts he has given to us in and through Jesus Christ by means of the Holy Spirit who tells us these things in God's holy word. As Albrecht Peters writes in his work *Creed*, "true faith is nothing other than complete reliance upon God the Almighty who is also our father who has given us his only begotten son Jesus Christ for the forgiveness of sins."[12] How we know about this message is by the work of the Spirit in word and sacrament.

Science does not have all the answers. However, Scripture has all that we need for life and godliness. Scripture tells us the story of origins: Where we come from. Who we are. How we came to being. Science guesses at all of this and tells us chemical compositions and possibilities. I remember when I was in Junior High School that we were taught that if we had a hypothesis we had to be able to repeat the experiment. Science has not been able to repeat

---

12. Peters, "Luther's Understanding of the Apostles' Creed," 60.

the origins of our universe without using any component parts. Scripture teaches us that God spoke the world into being. No scientist has yet to duplicate this event though they posit all types of theories.

When in discussions with atheists or those who believe in the scientific theory of evolution, I do not stay on that track of thought. Why? Simple. Scientists don't know everything and I know even less about the topic. What I do know is that God created the heavens and the earth. It is crucial when in these apologetic discussions that you don't get in over your skis. Don't get into parts of the conversation that you have no real knowledge of. Just as I've said to stay off your personal testimony, stay off your opinions and keep bringing in the word of God. Let me repeat what I've said previously: the gospel is the power of God unto salvation. You've got to get them back onto Scripture. If they want to know what you believe, stay on Scripture guided by the succinct parts of the Apostles' Creed. This is the track you must remain on in your conversations.

What Do We Know About God? Who Is He? What Has He Done?

These are the things that we know because he has informed us about himself in the Bible both in the Old and New Testaments. What does it tell us about him? What should we be telling others about him? Once again, stay on what you know from God's own word.

First, he is the all-powerful, all sovereign, all-knowing, all loving Creator of heaven and earth. This is who you are proclaiming by using the Creed. You are not proclaiming a God far off but the One who is very near and in Jesus Christ. This power is best displayed in the resurrection of Jesus Christ, of which we have hundreds of eyewitness accounts. We proclaim the One whose care over the world is seen in his giving his own son to die in our place. We learn from this Creed, as Luther says, that "none of us owns himself, nor can preserve his life or anything."[13]

How do we know God? We can only know him through his love for us through, his goodness towards us in giving us his beloved son Jesus Christ. Only in Jesus of Nazareth, the Risen One, can we ever know God the Father Almighty, Maker of Heaven and Earth. We don't merit this by our good works and yet as Father he offers Jesus to us simply out of love. Therefore,

---

13. Dau, *Concordia*, 328.

because God gave us his only Son we should love, praise, serve and obey him every day. We know God the Father through Jesus Christ his Son.

What Is It We're Answering in This Apologetic?

There is a tension in conversations about God that divides Creator from Father. What needs to be done as you are engaging in apologetics with an unbeliever is twofold: 1) Emphasize that because he created all things he remains Ruler over all, including you and I; 2) in order to know this Creator, Ruler, and Almighty Sovereign as loving Father, one must believe in his dear Son, Jesus Christ, who died, was buried, and rose again for the forgiveness of sins. As Luther emphasizes, "Since He is almighty, He is able to save. Since He is Father; He will do it."[14] Discussions of how God created all things should rely solely upon the accounts given in the Bible (Gen 1–3) while always remembering the gospel must be proclaimed even while giving an answer for the faith.

The reason we guide the conversations to the gospel is because it is the most important message in the universe: Jesus died, was buried, and rose again for the forgiveness of our sins. How do we know God as Father in this crazy, sin-sick world? This is a powerful message which we are to proclaim to people who are blind to the goodness of God and reject him because of all the abuses that they see in this world? When they ask you, "How can you believe in a loving God when people are so evil?" Answer: "Yes, this world is evil. But that's because we have rejected the Father Almighty who created this world. He rightly should be loved, honored, obeyed, and praised. We don't acknowledge him or thank him and we ought to. We should acknowledge his loving, fatherly heart when we escape all those negative things." Answering their negative questions with the blessings and the good things God has given us enables us then to move on to the next part of the Creed. Keep in mind that the goal of apologetics is not to get into areas that you know nothing about or are mere speculation. The goal is to proclaim the gospel of Jesus Christ to the person.

As you confess to them, "I believe in God the Father Almighty, Maker of Heaven and Earth" you must emphasize that he is your Father because of Jesus Christ. That you know he made heaven and earth and all things because he has said so in his word and that Jesus is the word of God (John 1:1). Steer away from endless speculations on topics that neither you nor

---

14. Peters, "Luther's Understanding of the Apostles' Creed," 60.

the skeptic have knowledge of. Never take on topics that you don't know. In the worst-case scenario simply respond, "May I get back to you on that?" and then do your due diligence to gain knowledge on that subject. This also serves as a good reason to bring the subject up again to continue the discussions. However, bring them back into the discussion of God as Father using his word since he promised that he would use it to bring many to true faith. Stay on what you know and the gospel of Jesus Christ.

It is in the second section of the Creed where we see how God the Father has given himself to us in Jesus Christ. We can find an overwhelming, unspeakable, eternal treasure and gift only through Jesus Christ his son who lived, died, was buried and rose again according to the Scriptures. It is so important that we maintain this as the message we proclaim. Therefore, the best way to show God as our Father, what we have received and what we owe in return, through the gift he gave us in his only begotten Son, Jesus Christ, is through our love and answering their questions honestly and with clarity.

The point of this section is not to get them to believe in God, per se, but in God the Father Almighty Maker of heaven and earth. We are not engaging in apologetics to get them to deism or some general "designer of the universe" view. No. We are engaging with them, defending what we believe about God the Father of our Lord Jesus Christ.

We are not engaging with them to discuss science. There are ample texts on various parts of science and theories out there and this book is not about engaging the inquisitor on theories but rather on the facts. I remember well the old police television show *Dragnet*, where sergeant Joe Friday would say, "Just the facts, ma'am." Well, that's what we are to be about. Evolution is about theories. The Bible is about facts. Stick to the facts and move the conversation as gently yet firmly as you can back on to the Bible.

Do you believe this? Do you believe he created all things out of nothing and spoke them all into existence by the word (Jesus)? Do you believe the creation account in Genesis 1–3 which tells us who he is and his love for sinner? It will be extremely difficult to say "I believe in God the Father Almighty, Maker of Heaven and earth" if it is not what you truly confess to believe. This is why we must continually go to the Scriptures and submit under them so that we may offer the unbeliever the word of life, the word by whom all things were made and are sustained.

In the nearly two decades in which I have been engaging in apologetics it has been the rare occasion in which the unbeliever came to me about my scientific knowledge but rather asking about Christianity, Jesus, the Bible, and why I believe in all of this. Neighbors, coworkers, friends, family, and those we interact with in society (clerks, cashiers, doctors, nurses, et al.) have come to me to ask what it is I believe and why. While sometimes the conversation may go into evolution, quantum physics, or mathematics in the origins of our universe, steering the conversation off of topics you may not know well and back onto the essentials of the faith is the task we are called upon to do. I have found that many Christians will discuss this amongst themselves but not so much with the unbeliever.

Engage with them on the essentials of the faith. Proclaim to them that Jesus died, was buried, and rose again according to the Scriptures and there are over five hundred eyewitnesses we can appeal to, and that he did this for the forgiveness of all of our sins. This is why we do apologetics. Debates can be fun and interesting but it has been shown they do not sway people as much as we think they might. Therefore, bring them the Word of Life (Jesus) through the words of life (the Bible) because it is him they truly need. Keep in mind that God's promise is not to bring people to faith through your personal testimony or your debating prowess but through the power of the Gospel.

What we are answering in apologetics is that *this* is what we believe. We do not doubt but echo the words of Martin Luther:

> This is most certainly true. God is Creator, the Almighty Maker of this world and as such He deserves obedience and worship. God is Father Almighty and as such deserves our love, praise, thanks and all our being. It is our duty to love God by loving our neighbor by defending the Christian faith and proclaiming the Gospel as we engage in apologetics.[15]

---

15. Dau, *Concordia*, 400.

Apostles' Creed Part 2

And in Jesus Christ, His only Son, our Lord,

Who was conceived by the Holy Spirit, born of the Virgin Mary,

Suffered under Pontius Pilate,

Was crucified, died and was buried.

He descended into hell.

The third day He rose again from the dead.

He ascended into heaven and sits at the right hand of God the Father Almighty.

From thence He will come to judge the living and the dead.

CHAPTER 6

And in Jesus Christ

THERE IS A LOT to tackle in the second part of the Apostles' Creed. So I decided to separate it into three chapters in this chapter I will be dealing with the title (Christ/Messiah), his Sonship and the term "Lord." It is in Jesus Christ that we are shown God the Father has withheld no good thing from us. It is this second part of the Apostles' Creed which in your apologetic discussions you will spend most of your time. While science and origins may be fabulous speculation or a topic of discussion it is not where you should spend your time. In the same way discussions on the end of the world or end times (eschatology) are the least known events since they have not occurred. Therefore, you need to stay off those topics as much as possible. When we get to discussions of end times (eschatology), in chapter 9, we will remain on what we do know from the Scriptures as written in the Creed.

As I have stated numerous times in this book the focus of the Creed is God. How do we know God? Through Jesus Christ who died, was buried, and rose again from the dead according to the Scriptures. Since we can only know God the Father through Jesus we try to remain on him in our discussions with unbelievers and skeptics. This section is also important to use when speaking with those who claim to be Christian and yet do not accept the triune God. In this second part of the Apostles' Creed the question that is answered is, "What do you believe about Jesus Christ?" This is the heart of the gospel. We do not believe in abstract ideas or teachings but in the actual and historical person of Jesus Christ and his work of redemption.

We now begin to look at the second part of the Creed. As shown in the previous chapter, in order to believe in God as Father, one must believe in Jesus Christ his only begotten son. In fact, it has been noted that you cannot know God as your Creator unless you know Jesus as your

Savior and Redeemer. The second part, as Dr. Martin, has stated, is the crucial part of the Apostles' Creed.[1] Jesus himself said that "He that hath seen me hath seen the father" (John 14:9). There is no way to know God the Father unless you know his Son. Therefore, we look at this second part of the Creed diligently because the message of the gospel that Jesus died, was buried, and rose again according to the Scriptures is the key which must be presented in any apologetic.

An apologetic that delves into science or the skeptics' questions which are not based and rooted in God's word results in many a rabbit trail to be followed. In fact those rabbit trails often result in rabbit holes from which you can barely dig yourself out, let alone get the unbeliever out of. I will repeat here that the goal of apologetics is to remove obstacles so that you may bring an unbeliever to the Door of salvation at the house of salvation, as Dr. Montgomery has stated, so that they may believe in Jesus Christ and have their sins forgiven. This is why I emphasize that you remain on the Scriptures because the word of God is the word of life. Jesus is that word of life. Therefore within your discussions, debates, and/or defense of the faith never leave it there but always include the proclamation of the gospel and of the fact that Jesus died, was buried, and rose again for the forgiveness of all our sins.

And in Jesus . . .

So the question that is asked is, who is Jesus? This is what is asked most by non-Christians. This is what they want to know and understand. They will ask you about him, in various ways, because this man has had more books written about him than any other person in history. This man divides time between BC and AD. This is who the Old Testament prophets foretold would come to be the Lamb that would take away the sins of the world and who the New Testament evangelists proclaimed to be both Lord and God in a hostile world. Jesus is the reason we believe. Jesus is the content of our belief. Jesus is the point of the Bible. Jesus is the reason why we are assured of heaven and our being raised from the dead. Jesus is the reason we have hope in a hopeless world. Jesus is the reason we love God and serve our neighbor because he first loved us. Jesus's death, burial, and resurrection is the reason we both defend and proclaim to the world the good news (gospel) of the forgiveness of sins. No one else matters in history but Jesus. Nothing else matters in this

---

1. Dau, *Concordia*, 400.

world except the good news that Jesus died for the sins of the world and rose again conquering death, hell, and the grave.

Many people have tackled who this Jesus is and responded in various ways with their own opinions: radical, martyr, good teacher, good man, miracleworker, liar, lunatic, false teacher, mystic, philosopher, magician, teacher of morality, spiritualist, reformer—and so much more. The evangelists, who lived with him and were eyewitnesses to the historic events of his life, listened and learned under his teaching for three years, having a very different view based on facts and not opinion. The New Testament proclaims that this Jesus of Nazareth is God-made-flesh, suffering servant, victorious king, and conqueror of death, Lamb of God to be sacrificed, Second Adam, Messiah, and Lord over all who holds everything together. They remind us that the very name Jesus was given because he will save his people from their sins. The evangelists teach us that he is the Christ (Anointed One of God), only Son of the Creator and Risen One who conquered death, hell, and the grave and is ascended and sits at the right hand of God.

C. S. Lewis posited three possibilities regarding who Jesus is in his work *Mere Christianity*. This argument, while not a perfect one in my opinion, certainly tackles the majority positions held by unbelievers and skeptics alike. Lewis states that Jesus, in forgiving sins (on numerous occasions), either knowingly does so as Son of God (Lord) or perhaps he was confused or even insane (lunatic) or purposefully deceived the people (liar).

Here in Matthew 9 we find that Jesus comes straight out and forgives the sins of this man. When the religious leaders squawk at him, for "only God can forgive sins," Jesus, proving himself to be God, the Savior (which is what Jesus means), heals the man, which also proves he can forgive sins. This is who Jesus is, Savior who forgives us from our sins.

> "For which is easier, to say, 'Your sins are forgiven,' or to say, 'Rise and walk'? But that you may know that the Son of Man has authority on earth to forgive sins"—he then said to the paralytic—"Rise, pick up your bed and go home." And he rose and went home.
>
> And when Jesus saw their faith, he said to the paralytic, "Son, your sins are forgiven." (Mark 2:5)

This is Mark's account of the same story. From the start of that Gospel Jesus is introduced as the Christ who is the Son of God. The fact is that we call the Savior Jesus because, as Matthew recounts in his Gospel, "and you shall call his name Jesus, for he will save his people from their sins." (Matt 1:21). *This* is what the unbeliever and skeptic need to hear: salvation from their sins.

This text from Luke is regarding the "sinner" who comes in to a home where Jesus is eating and falls to her feet crying and wiping his feet with her hair and Jesus responds to her, saying, "Your sins are forgiven" (Luke 7:48). Jesus had a knack for upsetting the religious people of the day. Yet, when you present that Jesus is Savior to those who ask you for a reason for your faith, do they acknowledge their need of forgiveness? That they are sinners? Many with whom I've come into contact reject that they are not perfect and therefore need forgiveness but that is what we must tell them. Just as we need the forgiveness of our own sins they too need salvation.

Two other scriptures to keep in mind are the following:

> And when he saw their faith, he said, "Man, your sins are forgiven you." (Luke 5:20)

> And he said to him, "Truly, I say to you, today you will be with me in paradise." (Luke 23:43)

These remind us that Jesus is God, who alone can forgive sins. Therefore, when we say, "and in Jesus" we are saying that we believe there is forgiveness of sins offered in the One who is Savior. There is a direct connection between God as our Father and knowing and believing in Jesus. Luther writes: "We see what we have from God over and above the temporal goods mentioned before. We see how He has completely poured forth Himself and withheld nothing from us."[2] Here in Jesus, the Savior, God the Father Almighty, has given us more than what we need for body but that which we need most desperately for our eternal soul.

In your excursion down the apologetic path (which I hope you do often) there are two types of people you will meet amongst non-Christians: 1) those who realize they are sinners and are looking for a way to find comfort and 2) those who think they are just fine and don't "sin" and therefore don't need a Savior. The second type, as Luther stated, need the law proclaimed to them over and over, for it is there that conviction will begin to occur so that they become the first type, those who recognize they are sinners in need of salvation. The first types, those already realizing they are sinners, need the gospel offered to them as the medicine for the soul. In your conversations with them, probing questions about evil in this world and then their own faults, failures, and feebleness to be

---

2. Dau, *Concordia*, 405.

perfect before God the Father Almighty, Maker of heaven and earth, will expose which type of person they are. However, both need Jesus; it will simply be the amount of time spent in the law of God that will determine the apologetic track you will take.

For the ones in the first category, I will call them "religious explorer" (though they are often called "seekers" Scripture states there are none who seek him [see Romans 3:11]) are wondering what you believe and should they become a Christian as well. These are the non-Christians who are curious about religion as a whole and are trying to find comfort, or as Saint Augustine said, that which fills the hole in their hearts. Presenting Jesus as the One who forgives their sins and as Savior is critical. Utilizing the accounts given in the Gospels of real, historical, and actual people who also sought forgiveness will bring with it an emphasis that Jesus is the Savior and that he has the power to forgive their sins. You may, at this point, share how you know your sins are forgiven through his word and the sacrament of baptism (not your decision, choice, or having raised your hand in some revival/evangelical service or summer camp). Make sure that you continue to focus on the fact that the very name this child was given, revealed to Joseph through the angelic message, is the very definition of Savior for that is what Jesus means.

Returning to C. S. Lewis, you may ask, why should it be so important to understand that Jesus is God himself who is not only saying he forgives sins but able to actually do it? If I say that Jesus is God to my non-Christian contact, how does that advance both the defense and then proclamation of the faith? Keep in mind, dear reader, that the point of apologetics is to get past any hurdles they may have to belief and bring them to that One who is the Door of salvation at the house of salvation. If Jesus is not God in human flesh, then he neither had the right nor ability to offer the forgiveness of sins to anyone. He is either, as you will read below, a lunatic or a liar, but he would not be Lord and that, my friends, would leave us in our sins and most miserable.[3]

Jesus does not sit on an even keel with Siddhartha Gautama (Buddha) or Mohammed or any other religious leader. He stands above even the prophets of the nation of Israel, King David, and the angels. The writer to the Hebrews states emphatically that Jesus is above all who came before and will come after. "For to which of the angels did God ever say, 'You are my Son, today I have begotten you?'" (Heb 1:5). Jesus is the Savior of the

---

3. See chapter 2 of this book for the famous quote by C. S. Lewis.

world and from whom you must, in your defense of the Christian faith, differentiate all who came before or might come after him.

So, who is this Jesus? Well, he's not a lunatic or a liar. God's word reminds us that Jesus is the perfect penalty, the Lamb, slain for the sins of the world. He bore the sins of all and paid for them so that we may have forgiveness and new life. Jesus, Savior, came and "redeemed me from sin, from the devil, from death, and from all evil."[4] What proves that this man is Savior? His resurrection, but I'll get to that in the next chapter.

This is who he is and whom you must continually point to because nowhere else is there true comfort nor the forgiveness of our sins. Only through Jesus can we know God as both Father and Maker of heaven and earth. Only through Jesus, "who will save us from our sins," can we possibly know forgiveness, be granted a new heart and eternal life. No matter the challenge put before you to discuss other religious figures, come back to the fact that his very name tells us exactly who he is: Savior.

Christ

As I began to prepare for writing this section on the Second Article I was overwhelmed with the number of times the term "Christ" is used in the New Testament. "Christ Jesus" is used by the apostle Paul over eighty times and "Jesus Christ" is used over one hundred forty times in the Gospels and remaining New Testament books. This term in the Greek is *Christos* and means "Anointed One." Israel believed the prophets and kings were anointed by God to their specific offices but they awaited the One who was to come as *the* Anointed One of God. This is who Jesus, our Savior, is: set apart by God to die for the world.

The question sometimes asked is why we called Jesus Christ. I want to take you to Matthew's Gospel, where Peter confesses Jesus as the Christ. When Jesus asks him "Who do people say that the Son of Man is?" (cf. Matt. 16) Peter gives a variety of answers. However, when Jesus directly asks Peter "Who do you say that I am?" Peter replies, "You are the Christ, the Son of the living God." This is such an important section of the Gospel of Matthew and in fact you will find a similar account in both the Gospels of Mark and Luke. As we know, the truth that Jesus is the Christ can only be revealed through the word by God's Holy Spirit.

---

4. Dau, *Concordia*, 401.

Faith confesses that Jesus is the anointed one, the Christ, the son of the living God. Therefore, this is what we proclaim. Jesus is the one sent by the Father into a sinful world to die so all who believe in him may have eternal life. Apart from this message there is no hope. Therefore in our proclamation and defense of the faith, giving reasons for why we believe, we must always have Jesus Christ as the central theme of our conversations. True faith comes through the hearing and hearing by the word of God (Rom 10:17). In order for the unbeliever with whom you are talking to be given faith, it is either going to be granted through the word and waters of baptism, or with an adult, through the preached and proclaimed the word of God. When the adult convert comes to their water baptism they will enter in on all the blessings that God has given in his promises through Jesus Christ.

Only Son

As shown in chapter 1, to the early creeds, calling Jesus God's only son was critical to the confession of faith. The early church wanted to make sure that there was a distinction between Jesus and those who believe in him who are made sons of God, adopted into his family, by grace through faith. Jesus is the Son of God the Father, Maker of heaven and earth, and in fact in the Gospel of John we read that Jesus is the Word of God and all things were made through him (cf. John 1:1–3). Jesus was not a created being but the uncreated only Son of the living God. He came and was made flesh so that he could bear the sins of the world in order that we might become the sons of God.

The Creed says we believe in Jesus Christ, his only Son. Once again the distinction is clear that our sonship with God is because of Jesus Christ and being adopted into the family of God, the household of faith. When you are talking to an unbeliever sometimes they may conjoin our sonship with Jesus so we need to correct them gently by making the distinction which the Creed does in saying "his only Son." In our defense of the faith we remind the inquirer or skeptic that Jesus is the only son of God because he is God incarnate, in the flesh. We are brought into the family but before we believe Jesus we are children of the devil. God the Father adopts us into his family because Jesus died in our place and is therefore, our elder brother. In this way we are explaining our relationship to God the Father, Maker of heaven and earth, through Jesus Christ, his only Son our Lord

AND IN JESUS CHRIST

Our Lord

"Jesus is Lord!" (Rom 10:8). This text is what Paul says to the Roman churches when he's talking about what their confession must be. Many have believed that this statement "Jesus Christ his only son" is an extension of that short confession. In the early ancient church, calling Jesus the Lord could very well be your death sentence by either Roman or Jewish leaders. In the very first sermon from Peter that we have recorded in the book of Acts his exhortation is "let all the house of Israel therefore know for certain that God has made him both Lord and Christ, this Jesus whom you crucified." (Acts 2:36) For Christians in the early church, to yield sole allegiance and obedience to the crucified and risen Jesus of Nazareth could result in arrest, torture and death. Calling Jesus Lord is not nearly the title but recognition that he is above all things and master of all King of kings.

> Therefore God has highly exalted him and bestowed on him the name that is above every name so that at the name of Jesus every knee should bow, in heaven and on earth and under the earth, and every tongue confess that Jesus Christ is Lord, to the glory of the father.[5]

How did Jesus demonstrate that he is above all things? Through his life and death and resurrection. Scripture teaches us that he raised himself from the dead. That is evidence of his being Lord over all. This is who we honor, trust, obey, love, and owe everything to. Bringing out this fact of his resurrection is bringing to the unbeliever the sweet gospel of salvation.

Martin Luther in his Large Catechism says this regarding the term Lord

> The little word of the Lord means simply the same as Redeemer. It means the one who has brought us from Satan to God, from death to life, from sin to righteousness, and who preserves us in the same.[6]

This is where we can explain how Jesus is our Savior. When I was Dutch Reformed Jesus was not the Savior of the world even though that's what the Bible plainly teaches. So proclaiming Christ to an unbeliever was not something I involved myself in because I didn't know whether or not Jesus died for them. Yet understanding what the Bible teaches I can say

---

5. Engelbrecht et al., "Philippians 2:9-11," 2035.
6. Dau, *Concordia*, 398.

to them this is how much it costs God the Father, Maker of heaven and earth, to pay for your salvation: Jesus died, was buried, and rose again. Jesus came from heaven to earth, conceived without sin so that he might overcome sin, die for our sins, and be raised again for our justification. Jesus has satisfied the righteous judgment of God the Father so that if you believe in him you will have eternal life.

Jesus didn't do this for himself. He did this for you and for me. When Jesus rose from the dead, death was conquered. What a fabulous message of hope in a world that is in sin where death reigns. Right now they are bound under the work of sin, death, and the devil and they need to hear the life-giving words of this great gift of salvation through Jesus Christ, our Lord.

As we use the Apostles' Creed to help guide us in our apologetic discussions we must always remember that it is the gospel which is the power of God for salvation. It is the proclaiming of the life, death, burial, and resurrection of Jesus Christ. This is alone the message of hope for those dying apart from him. Jesus alone is able to save. The Father has given his son so that none need to remain in their sins separated from God and forever cast out from his blessings. Utilizing the statements in the Creed, understanding each part that we confess, for many of us, weekly, enables us to present this most precious gift to those in desperate need of the forgiveness of their sins. The Creed offers us a structure and a way to remember the key essential facts of the Christian faith. As we progress in our study on using the Creed for both proclamation and defense of the faith we will begin with Christ's humiliation and end with his exultation.

CHAPTER 7

Born to Die

Jesus's Humiliation Part 1

WHAT IS MEANT BY Jesus's humiliation? It simply means that God the Son willingly put aside all the privileges indeed. Saint Paul, in his letter to the Philippians, says, "though he was in the form of God, [he] did not count equality with God a thing to be grasped, but made himself nothing, taking the form of a servant, being born in the likeness of men. And being found in human form, he humbled himself by becoming obedient to the point of death, even death on a cross" (Phil 2:6–11). Since Jesus is fully God he then took on being fully man. This is what we mean by his humiliation. He stepped out of eternity into time, being born of the Virgin Mary and taking on human flesh, becoming servant of all.

Conceived and Virgin Birth

Why are we confessing how Jesus was born? What is so important about it? How does this fit our defending the Christian faith? These are some of the questions we may be asking ourselves about the birth narratives of Jesus Christ our Lord. I have learned that the importance of an event is sometimes weighted by the amount of time the recorders of those events spend on it. The Gospel of Matthew spends the first two chapters on the birth and infancy of Christ while the Gospel of Luke spends two chapters on the birth and early years of Christ.

There is a general outline which both Matthew and Luke use from the angel's announcements to both Mary and Jesus along with a visit to Mary's cousin Elizabeth and how this connects Jesus to the prophecies of the Old Testament. In Matthew, Joseph is prominent, being warned about

Mary's pregnancy and then, after the birth, the rage of King Herod. The angel warns him to take the child and his mother to Egypt. Luke focuses on Mary's role as the Virgin who has conceived the holy one and that she is to call his name Jesus. In Matthew Joseph is also told by the angel to call his name Jesus.

There are numerous prophecies from the Old Testament that are very notable and should be memorized. Here is a list:

- Matthew 1:23 cites Isaiah 7:14
- Matthew 2:6 cites Micah 5:2
- Matthew 2:15 cites Hosea 11:1
- Matthew 2:8 cites Jeremiah 31:15
- Matthew 2:23 uses the term "Nazarene" which is close to the Hebrew word for branch in Isaiah 11:1.

These passages would be excellent for all of us to memorize from both the Old and New Testaments because often you will speak with someone who wants to know whether or not Jesus's birth was foretold. The New Testament writers were connecting Jesus with fulfillment of prophecy and are one reason we can call him both anointed or the Christ as well as our Lord.

Often when defending the faith the skeptic or unbeliever may say, "these are just myths and fairytales." How do we defend against this? We bring in history. And Luke lists the historical genealogy for Jesus, one from the line of Mary the other from the line of Joseph. Luke furthermore gives a historical context by bringing in the lineage and the names of those ruling the empire and local areas. What do I mean by this? He gives us the names of officials at the time of Jesus's birth, such as Quirinius as the governor of Syria and Caesar Augustus as the ruler of the Roman Empire. The governor of Syria held a census twice in each of his terms of service. The documents of these are available for inspection and prove that he was the governor during the time of Jesus's birth. Very often Luke gives us the historical context for events in the life of Jesus and these are very useful in our apologetic method.

The Gospel of Mark begins with the story of Jesus and his baptism by John. The Gospel of John also talks about the Spirit in his recounting of Jesus's baptism in water. So how does this fit in the creedal statement "who was conceived by the Holy Spirit, born of the Virgin Mary"? While Matthew and Luke show the Holy Spirit involved in the conception of

Jesus directly, in John's count we see the Holy Spirit at the beginning of Jesus is ministry. Mark writes that at Jesus's baptism he "saw the heavens torn apart and the Spirit descending like a dove on him" (1:10) while the author of John testifies, "I saw the Spirit descending from heaven like a dove, and it remained on him" (1:32).

Mary asked the angel how this could be. Our friends, family, coworkers, and neighbors may also wonder how Jesus could be conceived in Mary by the Holy Spirit. The *how* is not for us to answer. However, the *why* is. How this happened is truly a miracle prophesied by Isaiah centuries earlier. We don't know how this was done and it does not matter, it only matters that it was done. The Heidelberg Catechism explains why Jesus needed to be both God and man in quite an easy way to remember. Jesus needed to be fully man to represent humanity and fully God to withstand the very wrath of God against a sinful human. Saint Paul writes in Romans that as in Adam all have died and death has spread to all men because all sinned. Paul also reminds us that Adam was a "type of the one who was to come" (5:12, 14b). That is not where Paul leaves us, for he then says

> But the free gift is not like the trespass. For many died through one man's trespass, much more at the grace of God in the free gift by the grace of that one man Jesus Christ abounded for many. In the free gift is not like the result of that one man's sin. . . . For it, because of one man's trespass, death reigned through that one man, much more will those who receive the abundance of grace and the free gift of righteousness reign in life through the one man Jesus Christ. (Romans 5:15-17)

Martin Luther in his explanation of the Creed in his Small Catechism asks, "What does this mean? Answer: I believe that Jesus Christ, true God, begotten of the father from eternity, and also true man, born of the Virgin Mary, is my Lord."[1] In his Larger Catechism Luther talks about how much it cost Jesus and what he spent and risked so that he might win us and bring us under his dominion. He further elaborates that Jesus became man (John 1:14), was conceived and born without sin (Heb 4:15), from the Holy Spirit and from the Virgin Mary (Luke 1:35), so that he might overcome sin. Once again I encourage you that in your defense of the faith or proclamation of the Creed you emphasize all aspects of Jesus Christ.

In fact Martin Luther says at the close of this work that "the entire gospel that we preach is based on this point that we properly understand

---

1. Dau, *Concordia*, 405.

this article is that upon which our salvation and all our happiness rests."[2] People are clamoring for happiness. I remember in the seventies the little happy-face buttons and the song "don't worry be happy." Where can they find happiness their rest? Certainly they will not find it in this world. Yes, we must point them to Jesus Christ. That his birth, which is uncontrollable by the infants conceived, was foretold so many centuries before it happened is one basis or point of defense. We cannot show them a Christ without showing them the words of Christ through the Scriptures. This is why I encourage you to continue utilizing the Creed and the Scriptures that explain why we have these phrases in the Creed.

Conclusion

Very often unbelievers want to know why we believe what we believe and challenge its veracity. We must be prepared with Scripture, our confessions, and the historical evidence for the birth, life, ministry, death, burial, and resurrection of Jesus Christ. We are told by Peter in his letter to the Christians, who had been dispersed throughout the Roman Empire because of persecution, that when someone asks you the reason for your faith you must have an apologetic, a defense, an answer that will both defend and proclaim the one true faith, Christianity. It does us no good to be ill-equipped in a battle for the eternal lives of your friends, family, neighbors, coworkers, and even strangers who may come knocking at your door. We must offer the greatest gift: Jesus Christ, his only Son, our Lord, who was conceived by the Holy Spirit, born of the Virgin Mary.

---

2. Dau, *Concordia*, 405.

CHAPTER 8

For You

Suffered, Crucified and Died

I WANT TO BEGIN with the suffering that Jesus underwent. What actually happened on that Roman cross, the main form of execution during the Roman Empire? The Mayo Clinic did a medical study into what happens on a Roman cross. There is clearly nothing pleasant about a crucifixion. However, having an understanding of it helps us to understand what Jesus went through on the day of his death. This study was published in the *Journal of the American Medical Association* in 1989.[1] So let me do a little history.

When did crucifixion begin? In their study they found that it probably began first with the Persians (modern-day Iran) where initially, the victim was suspended to keep their feet from touching the ground. Later on the Phoenicians, traders to many lands, also acquired this practice and spread it to other cultures including the Greeks. Alexander the Great introduced the practice in Corinth where it would be later picked up by the Romans. The Romans began to use the cross as a form of execution around the time of Jesus's birth.

The Trial and Flogging

What was the purpose for this type of execution? We can call it the maximization plan. The first reason or purpose was to maximize the pain and secondly the disgrace. The Romans perfected crucifixion as a punishment designed to maximize pain and suffering and it wasn't really about killing

---

1. See "Crucifixion" and Edwards et al., "On the Physical Death of Jesus Christ," for the historical information in this chapter.

the person quickly. Rather it was about executing the prisoner in a horrific manner in order to put fear into their subjects' hearts. The whole process of crucifixion brought about severe pain and could last days. Secondly it was to maximize the disgrace because Rome will want to emphasize that the worst of the worst was being executed in this way. It was also notable that a Roman citizen, unless they were a deserter or traitor, would never be crucified. This form of execution was reserved for slaves, foreigners, revolutionaries, and vile criminals.

What Jesus underwent after his arrest was typical for a Roman crucifixion. First, the criminal would undergo flogging or scourging. This was intended to bring the victim to a state just short of death. The whip used had iron balls, or jagged metal, or even bones tied a few inches from the end of each leather thong. While the iron balls would cause deep bruising the leather would cut into the skin. If the whip had metal and bones tied to it then it would cut through skin, muscles, and to the bone.

After the flogging, the victim would carry his own cross bar (*patibulum*) from the flogging area inside the city to the crucifixion area outside the city walls. A crucifixion was always held outside the city because the process was horrible and disturbing to the citizens. The upright of the cross (*stipe*) was permanently mounted on the crucifixion area. The part that the victim carried was the cross bar and weighed anywhere from 75 to 125 pounds. The victim would have to balance the cross bar on their shoulders while their arms were tied to it. In this position, if the victim tripped or fell, they could not use their arms to break their fall and would likely fall face first into the ground. The victim was often escorted by a Roman guard, most likely a sentry and with several soldiers, who were responsible for guarding the victim until his death. One of the soldiers would then write out the crimes and nail that above the victim's head on the upper right beam.

Roman Cross

Once the crucifixion area was reached, the victim would be offered a drink of wine mixed with myrrh to act as a mild painkiller. We see this being done in Mark's account when Jesus has been nailed to the cross (15:23). The victim would be nailed to the cross bar. The nails would be driven through the wrists, not through the palms, as these are unable to support the body weights of the person. The feet would be nailed to the upright post.

Once crucified, the victim could live for a period ranging from a few hours to a few days. How long they lived depended upon how severe the flogging or scourging was. Once the victim died, if no one claimed the body, it would be left on the cross to be eaten by predatory animals. Family could claim the body for burial. When they did, a Roman soldier would pierce the chest with a sword or spear to ensure the victim was actually dead.

So what actually kills in a crucifixion? The scourging was to weaken the victim and cause massive blood loss and most likely induced shock. By the time the victim had carried the cross bar to crucifixion area they would be exhausted. On the cross the victim would have breathing difficulties. Because the victim would have their body weight suspended by their arms this position makes it nearly impossible to completely ask for help. The victim would be able to take shallow breaths for a while but eventually would be forced to push himself up by his feet in order to take in a full breath. This of course would exacerbate the pain because he's on feet that have been nailed to the upright bar.

So in a crucifixion there are three aspects that we need to remember when talking about the physical suffering of Jesus Christ. The victim's weight is fully supported by his feet. The nails through the feet have likely hit two major nerves running through the area. This results in excruciating pain in the legs. The nails in the wrists have likely pierced the main nerve running through the arm and as the victim pushed up to breathe the wrists would rotate against the nail irritating the nerve and causing intense pain in the arms. Some of the medical researchers also believed that crucifixion could dislocate the shoulders or elbows making any movement aggravate the pain from these injuries. Thirdly, the wounds on the victims back from the flogging were up against the rough part of the upright post and tended to reopen the wounds leading to more pain and blood loss. The combination of all three would quickly force the victim to lower himself back down. Eventually, the victim would no longer be able to raise himself up and they would suffocate. The shock from blood loss due to the scourging would hasten this process. However, if it took too long for the victim to die, the legs would be broken to finish them off. This would prevent the victim from being able to raise himself up and he would suffocate in a manner of minutes.

So then what happened to Jesus on the cross? All of these torturous points that I just reviewed did happen to Jesus, except that he died without them breaking his leg bones. The skeptic will often say that Jesus didn't really die he might have just been in a coma. The Islam skeptic has been taught two different theories: first, that Jesus's body was swapped with someone who looked like him and secondly, that he didn't die but was in a coma and recovered in the tomb. So it is important that we look at the biblical text for what happened to Jesus on the cross. As stated previously in this book, the eyewitness testimony of the evangelists is perfectly reliable because these things actually occurred within their own personal knowledge, as Simon Greenleaf has stated.

To get a general overview we know from the account in Matthew 26:26–29 that Jesus spent the last hours before the crucifixion in several places in Jerusalem. He started the evening in the upper room in southwest Jerusalem and then went to the garden of Gethsemane. He was then arrested and brought back to the palace of the high priest where he was questioned by analysts, a former high priest, and Caiaphas, Annas's son-in-law. Afterwards, he was tried by the Sanhedrin, found to be guilty of blasphemy by proclaiming himself the Son of God. He was sentenced to the death penalty—however, only the Romans were able to execute criminals. So he was sent to Pontius Pilate at the Antonia fortress. Pilate, not finding anything wrong, sends Jesus to King Herod, who returned him back to Pilate. Pilate then submits to the pressure of the crowds and orders that Jesus be flogged and crucified. Jesus is finally led out of the city to be crucified on Golgatha.

It is reasonable to assume that Jesus was in good health prior to the ordeal that he was going to face in the hours before his death. Having been a carpenter and traveling throughout the land during his ministry would have required that he be in good physical condition walking everywhere. Right before the crucifixion, however, he was forced to walk over two and a half miles over a sleepless night, during which he suffered great anguish through his six trials, where he was mocked, ridiculed, and severely beaten.

There is also the mental anguish which we know Jesus suffered because when he was praying he swept great drops of blood. While in Gethsemane, Jesus is betrayed by Judas and arrested by the Jews (Matt 26). His disciples all desert him, even at the expense of running away naked (Mark 14:51–52). Jesus is then bound (John 18:12) and brought back to the city to the court of the high priest, which is located near the upper room. There is a huge issue of the witnesses who spoke against Jesus that probably caused even more mental torment.

While in the court of the high priest, he is questioned (John 18:13, 19) and struck by a soldier (John 18:22). He is then brought to Caiaphas and the Sanhedrin who sought to put him to death based on the false testimony of many witnesses. The major issue with the witnesses who were brought against him is that they did not agree. However, by the law, no one could be put to death without the agreement of two or three witnesses (Deut 19:15; 17:6). Although the witnesses do not agree, Jesus is found guilty of blasphemy when he tells them his identity as the Son of God (John 18:19–24). He is then sentenced to death and is ridiculed by the palace guards who spit on him, beat him, and slap him in the face (Mark 14:65). We also know that during the trial Peter denies him three times (Luke 22:56–62). Jesus is then brought back to Pilate who flogs him (John 19:1) and a crown of thorns is placed on his head and they put a purple robe on him (John 19:2).

There were other issues with Jesus's arrest. The time and date of the trial were illegal because it took place at night and on the eve of the Sabbath, and a half a Sabbath, as it was Passover. The Sanhedrin had no authority to instigate charges only to investigate supposed charges brought before it. However in Jesus's trial the court itself formulated the charges. These charges were also changed during the trial from blasphemy to revolutionary. The Sanhedrin also falsely charged him with not paying taxes to the Roman Empire. The use of two witnesses, as required by the law, also was not followed because no two witnesses agreed. Furthermore, Christ is not permitted a defense which under the Jewish law required an exhaustive search into the facts presented by witnesses. The Sanhedrin were not allowed to convict or put death sentence into effect (John 18:31). However, this is just what they did. Because they could not carry it out they brought Jesus to Pilate.

There is a lot of prophecy being fulfilled in the suffering, crucifixion, and death of Jesus Christ. This is important to show the skeptic that these events didn't just happen because Jesus's plan went awry. Instead we need to show them this was God's plan all along. The significance of the scarlet/purple robe (Matthew 27:28 writes scarlet while Mark 15:17 and John 19:2 state purple and Luke 23:11 simply writes of a "robe") and crown of thorns is to emphasize that Jesus took on himself the sins of the world (Gen 3:17–18). Thus, the articles that Jesus wore to his crucifixion heading to the hill of Golgotha are symbols to show that Jesus took on the sins and the curse of the world.

Died and was Buried

The Gospels don't give us every single detail of the beating that Jesus withstood heading to the cross. However, in the book of Isaiah (50:6–8; 52:13–14) we are given a glimpse of what happened. We read that his beard was pulled out and that the beating was so severe that he no longer looked human. People were appalled to look at him his disfigurement was so massive and it might explain why he was not easily recognized in his post-resurrection appearances. From beating he was then led to be crucified on the hill of Golgotha.

The beatings were so severe along with the floggings that Jesus was unable to carry the cross. Many theorize that he fell while going down the road to Golgotha. We do know from the account in Luke 23 that Simon of Cyrene was summoned to help carry the cross beam.

Since it was preparation day (that is, the day before the Sabbath) the Jewish leaders wanted the bodies of all the criminals there to be taken down. This meant that the soldiers would have to expedite fission by breaking the legs of the crucified. Joseph of Arimathea, a prominent member of the Council, who was himself waiting for the kingdom of God, went boldly to Pilate and asked for Jesus's body. Jesus had already died. In the Gospel of John (19:31–22) Pilate is surprised that Jesus is already dead. As mentioned previously crucifixion was a long drawn-out death. And still Pilate orders that the soldiers make sure he really is dead. When the apostle John gives his account he notes that when the soldier pushed the spear into Jesus's side that both water and blood came flowing out. The Mayo Clinic notes this is pleural and pericardial fluid from the sack around Jesus's heart that had burst at his death and had accumulated in the chest cavity around the lungs. This is a definitive proof that Jesus had died.

Jesus's body is then wrapped in linen as we read in Matthew's account of the burial of Jesus. This wrapping was done tightly around the whole body from head to toe. We actually see this in the account of the resurrection of Lazarus since he had to be unbound when Jesus raised him from the dead (John 12). The women along with Joseph of Arimathea and Nicodemus bring a mix of spices roughly seventy-five pounds (John 19:39). Since the religious leaders were very concerned that the disciples would steal Jesus's body they requested from Pilate to have a guard outside the tomb. They said to Pilate, "Sir, we remember how that imposter said, while he was still alive, after three days I will arise." Pilate's responds to them by saying "Go, make it as secure as you can" (Matt 27:62–66).

The guard set by the Sanhedrin works to provide compelling evidence for the resurrection. Historically a "guard" was upward of a dozen soldiers all under penalty of death for either sleeping on duty or walking away from their post. God permitted this to happen so the disciples, and all believers, may have confidence that the resurrection was not a hoax, an elaborate scheme or hallucination, but fact.

Jesus died on the Roman cross of execution and was buried for the forgiveness of our sins.

CHAPTER 9

Why the Resurrection Matters

> The apostles made this proclamation not as a beautiful story, but as something which actually happened. The uniqueness of the Christian faith consists in the fact that it was founded on a unique historical event. —Sir Norman Anderson
>
> If Christ was not raised, then *all* our preaching is useless, and your trust in God is useless —1 Cor 15:14 (my emphasis)

WE NOW COME TO the most crucial part of the Christian faith: the historic and physical resurrection of Jesus Christ. As Sir Norman Anderson said, this was "something which actually happened."[1] We are not telling myths or fairy tales but actual history recorded by actual people who were eyewitnesses to the events. No other religion in the world has a founder who rose again from the dead three days later. Every other single religion has a burial and or a memorial site for their leader who is still dead. Christianity alone rises far above every other religion, philosophy, and worldview because Jesus Christ has risen from the dead. This is what gives us a sure confidence.

In a world where death is seen everywhere from plantlife to animal life to friends, family, and neighbors both the unbeliever and the skeptic need a new life. Every single person in this world has been touched by death and because of that often fears death. We as Christians don't have to fear death because Jesus Christ has conquered death. We don't have to fear what is on the other side because we know the one who has come back from the other side. We alone, Christians, have the message of hope.

The Creed says:

> And in Jesus Christ, his only son, our Lord, who was conceived by the Holy Spirit, born of the Virgin Mary, suffered under Pontius

---

1. Anderson, *Christianity and Comparitive Religion*, 52.

Pilate, was crucified, died and was buried. He descended into hell. The third day he rose again from the dead.

Why does the Creed talk about his death and resurrection? As Luther explains in the second article of the Creed in his Larger Catechism,

> So that he (Jesus) might make satisfaction for me and pay what I owe . . . After that he rose again from the dead, swallowed up and he devoured death.[2]

He, Jesus Christ, who is our Lord and whom we believe in for the forgiveness of sins, has swallowed up death. According to the apostle John in his first letter (1 John 3:8) the reason the Son of God appeared was to destroy the works of the devil. Imagine, if you will, phrasing it this way, Christ, the destroyer of sin death and the devil. This is the message we have for those who come to us and ask the reason we believe in Jesus. No other religious leader can claim this. Every other religious leader taught how you could climb your way up to their God. However, you were never assured that you would actually obtain their version of paradise or eternal life. You can never know in those other religions if you've done enough. Sadly even with some Christian denominations you don't know if you've really done enough. However, in the biblical faith we know that Jesus paid the price for us by dying on the cross and rising on the third day for our justification (Rom 4:25). With this message we bring hope to the lost and to the dying, the Word of Life himself.

However before we get to the absolutely incredible news of the physical and historical resurrection of Jesus Christ it benefits us to better understand the suffering, crucifixion, death, and burial of our Lord and Savior. When we understand the two aspects of Jesus's death, his physical death and his payments of our penalty for sin (spiritual death) then we can answer their questions which may even be "Why did Jesus die?" explaining to them the requirements of God's law. Dr. Montgomery credits Luther with saying that for the person who does not recognize their sin, you need to present the law and then the Gospel. However to the person who comes to you who is under conviction of the law then you bring them the Gospel. Both situations need to see why Jesus died for them.

---

2. Dau, *Concordia*, 401, 405.

Jesus's Exaltation: Resurrection

If Christ is risen, nothing else matters.
And if Christ is not risen—nothing else matters.

—Jaroslav Pelikan

Pitied or Pivotal?

The resurrection is of vital importance to the Christian faith for without it there would be no transition from death to life for anyone. It is the critical event upon which *all* of Christianity stands on. If Jesus did not rise from the dead then we are to be pitied. Pitied! That is a pretty strong word. The world should feel sorry for us and have sympathy for us since we believe such a foolish thing could happen. We should be shamed at our gullibility at such a teaching if it did not happen. Consequently, the resurrection becomes the pivotal teaching of Christianity and must be declared when we are either proclaiming or defending the faith.

I begin with Paul using the term "pitied" because if you do not believe that Jesus rose again from the dead, physically, then you probably think that those who do should be pitied. In the great it also denotes being miserable. Imagine that! If we believe in the resurrection and it did not actually occur we should be miserable. Why? Because we've believed a lie which means, as Paul says, we are still in our sins and therefore in quite the miserable condition before God.

We Christians do not blindly believe this truth but I believe it because there is ample support for the fact that God did not leave his son in the grave but for our salvation and our justification did indeed raise him up on the third day physically. Well, that said, we should not blindly believe because as we read the testimony of the apostles, of Paul and even of Jesus's enemies and those who did not believe him, in the Scriptures, we find that this was the critical event, the pivotal point upon which Christianity stands or falls. See, Christians have history and eyewitness testimonies on our side. We have, as Paul said, over five hundred eyewitnesses that he told the Corinthians they could still talk to about them seeing the bodily risen Jesus. Paul's own defense of the faith before Agrippa and Felix is where he reminds them that the resurrection didn't happen in a corner.[3] It was actually something they all knew about and none had refuted it by producing a body or proving the disciples stole it. No, Paul says they know about this and they don't disagree.

Resurrection: Jesus's Claims to It

The very fact that Jesus predicts his own resurrection is astounding. No other religious leader or founder ever stated that they would rise from the dead. They stated they had direct revelations or visions, dreams and messages from God or an angel, but they never said if and when they died or were killed, three days later they would rise again. Islam, Hinduism, and Mormonism never claim their leaders or founders were God in human flesh or that they would raise themselves from the grave. The fact is Muslims visit the grave of Mohammed which evidences his mortality and humanity. Though Joseph Smith claimed that he would be there on judgment day with authority like Jesus, he never spoke of rising from the dead. Never was a miracle performed that other eyewitnesses saw which proved one day he could become a god. Yet, here were the disciples of Jesus, who just a short time before were cowering in a house, hiding from the authorities for fear of their own deaths, now loudly and publically proclaiming Jesus risen from the dead (cf. Acts 4:13). Every one of them, except the apostle John, would die by execution for their eyewitness testimony to the actual events.

Eyewitness Testimony

Defining Terms:

Objective: "Expressing or dealing with facts or conditions as perceived without distortion by personal feelings, prejudices, or interpretations."[4] It is based upon a set of facts which are verifiable through eyewitness testimony and documentary proof. An objective gospel proclamation then is based upon the evangelists' eyewitness testimony found in the documentary evidence of the four Gospels, Acts, and their Epistles over and above a personal testimony styled message.

---

3. See Acts 26.
4. "Define Objective," https://www.merriam-webster.com/dictionary/objective.

Subjective: peculiar to a particular individual: personal; modified or affected by personal views, experience, or background. Subjective testimonies are grounded in personal experience or personal perceptions.[5] With regard to gospel proclamation subjectivism merely expresses the feelings of the speaker, emphasizing them over the evidential proofs and statements of Scripture.

The apostle John, in writing to a local church, does not appeal to his personal experience which he had within him. Instead, just as Saint Paul did, he appeals to eyewitness testimony. He writes, "*We* proclaim to you what *we* have seen and heard" (1 John 1:1; emphasis added). Notice the use of the plural *we*. John's appeal is not to his personal inward experience or vision, but rather to a plurality of eyewitnesses. This appeal to eyewitness testimony is a strong argument for the truth of the event and should be emphasized when engaged in apologetic discussions.

The objective evidence we have is the eyewitness testimony of the evangelists' accounts in the gospels and the remainder of the apostles in the book of Acts. They were there during the life of Jesus. Again, as Peter and John write, they touched and ate with Jesus. Peter writes about his failure to defend Christ outside of where the trial took place while John testifies in his gospel about how he was there at the crucifixion when Jesus spoke to him about caring for his mother. These men, and Paul reminds us, over five hundred others, were then eyewitnesses of Jesus being raised from the dead. Eyewitness testimony which references the testimony of others is rather strong evidence and must not be discarded.

Christianity, as an objective faith, points to objective evidence instead of inward change. Yes, there is inward change in those who have come to faith in Christ but even that is insufficient to convince another that Christianity is true. Instead, Christians must not focus upon their feelings, testimony, or decision to trust Christ. Instead, they should zero in on the facts that we have in the Scripture given by eyewitnesses to the events at the time they happened.

---

5. "Define Subjective," https://www.merriam-webster.com/dictionary/subjective.

When Christians Speak of Their Own Subjective Evidences, Their Personal Testimony or Feelings the Result Is Devastating For the Gospel

Presenting a subjective gospel to the unbeliever is one way to lose the argument and ruin the defense of the faith. While other religions may rightly claim that they are the truth because of their feelings, opinions, and experiences, Christianity is not based upon the subjective but upon the factual eyewitness accounts by those who were there during the actual and historical events written in the gospels and the book of Acts. More than that, the one who may come to faith by a subjective testimony is going to look within their own personal experience for assurance of the faith instead of the factual testimony and that results in either despair or pride; as Rev. Wolfmueller says in his book *Has American Christianity Failed?*, "Enthusiasm (looking within for the move of God) is what drives the terrible swing between pride and despair that marks the life of most American Christians."[6]

The typical evangelical focus upon the subjective, which looks for God within, when proclaimed to another, results in that individual thinking this is the way to tell others about Jesus. While we all desire to see the inward work of God within the unbeliever, we cannot rely upon a subjective approach. Christians must see that focusing on the inward drives the unbeliever to look inward and desire to experience what they have rather than run to the cross and believe the gospel. Using this approach (subjective) one needs to ask, "What happens if they do not have this same experience?" It will drive them to despair. What if they have even more grandiose visions and experience? It will drive them to pride since God moves more mightily in them. This results in either a lack of assurance (despair) for the believer because experiences come and go or in lack of reliance upon God (pride).

Recently, I was in a discussion with a friend and shared that I no longer tell my conversion story, but instead simply speak about the day God converted me through his word. Specifically referencing the forgiveness of sins attained for us by the death and resurrection of Jesus and the Holy Spirit working through his word, 1 John 1:9–10 in my case, becomes the focus of proclamation. Once they begin to ask why I believe, then the conversation must switch from when I believed (subjective experience) to the objective truths of the gospel: Jesus died, was buried, and rose again

---

6. Wolfmueller, *Has American Christianity Failed?*, 22.

according to the Scriptures and was seen by all the apostles, Paul, and over five hundred other witnesses (cf. 1 Cor 15:1–4).

The despair that this type of proclamation brings is that it places the importance upon the experience of the recipient rather than that which Jesus Himself did. When that begins to stew, the new convert, lacking these experiences which the Christian had told them they would have as well, begins to doubt whether or not they are truly saved. This inward and subjective flaw is seen best in the multiple altar calls a Christian convert may attend just so that they make sure they are saved. Let's pray that God's Holy Spirit will use the word of God, which you are proclaiming as the defense of the Christian faith, to grant them a new heart of flesh and remove the heart of stone. Keep in mind that a subjective presentation results in a debilitated convert as well. How then do I use an objective presentation of the gospel?

Three Days

For three days Jesus was laid dead in a cold tomb. On the first day of the week as Mary Magdalene and the other Mary prepared more spices and began their journey to the tomb they expected to find Jesus's body still there. In fact none of his disciples expected the body to be missing and least of all for him to have been risen from the dead. The disciples have lost all hope as they watched their rabbi nailed to a Roman cross and killed.

"Greetings" is what Mary heard and she took hold of his feet and worshiped him. It was Jesus himself saying to her, "Do not be afraid; go and tell my brothers to go to Galilee, and there they will see me" (Matt 28:9–10). Certainly the report of the women was unbelievable to the disciples. You see Matthew 27:60 tells us a "large stone" had been placed over the entrance to the tomb. Unless Jesus had some help from within or the disciples overpowered the Roman guards from without, there is no way anyone moved that stone. The Roman guards at the tomb were given the job to guard it. Since there's been rumors that the body of Jesus might be stolen they were ready to meet their challenge. So who moved the stone? God did.

Some skeptics had said Jesus merely recovered in the tomb. However, think about this—if he recovered he'd be in pretty bad shape. He would have walked on wounded feet to travel to the disciples. Jesus had undergone six hours of trial, been beaten, then scourged with thirty-nine lashes which left his back raw, exposed, and bloodied. He had a crown of thorns forced on his head ripping his scalp, and was crucified with nails in the hands and feet. He hung there for six hours bleeding and was dehydrated. When his body was requested the soldiers confirmed that Jesus was dead which was evidenced by the emission of blood and water when they pierced his side with a spear. He was left in the tomb for three days without medical care tightly wrapped in burial shrouds. No one in that condition would be able to revive himself, sit up by himself, walk on those pierced feet, or single-handedly move the large stone with hands that were unusable due to the wrist piercings which severed the median nerve in the hands. In fact it really takes more to believe this then it does to believe the physical bodily resurrection of Jesus Christ from the dead.

Documentary Evidence

In Christianity we have been given documentary evidence. It is by evidence, verifiable, documentary and historical, that the skeptic is then challenged. You may be asking, "What is that documentary evidence?" It is the evangelists' account from Matthew through John and the book of the Acts of the Apostles. These were written by the disciples/apostles themselves or someone close to them who could give them the information and correct the accounts if they went awry.

Remember that apologetics is about removing the hurdles and reasons for unbelief bringing someone to the Door of salvation at the house of salvation. Once hurdles are removed then the unbeliever is brought to Christ as the only true Savior. However, when a Christian does not value the biblical evidence, instead relying upon a voice of God outside of the Scriptures, then it is akin to throwing the evidence into the trash heap. The Christian must recognize the value of such evidence, going through each document, some history, and, again, the eyewitness testimony the church has been given by the evangelists.

It does the Christian no use when they refuse to use of the evidence given in Scripture. In *Scaling the Secular City*, J. P. Moreland encourages Christians of all denominations to overcome their objections to using apologetics as one tool in the work of evangelism. He writes, "Apologetics is a ministry designed to help unbelievers over some intellectual obstacles and believers to remove doubts that hinder spiritual growth."[7] He likens the use of apologetics with the use of the sermon in this vein. Further he writes,

---

7. Moreland, *Scaling the Secular City*, 11.

> Apologetics can help remove obstacles to faith and thus aid unbelievers in embracing the gospel. Certainly the Holy Spirit must be involved in drawing men to Christ. But a preacher is not absolved of the responsibility of preparing his sermon just because the Spirit must apply the Word of God to the lives of his listeners. In the same way, ambassadors for Christ are not excused from the responsibility of defending the gospel. The Spirit can use evidence to convict men of the truth of the proclamation.[8]

While the argument is that utilizing any objective defense limits or replaces the work of the Holy Spirit, the Scriptures say differently. The apostle Peter states that when unbelievers or skeptics begin to question what we believe, we are to be prepared with an answer (*apologia*) and a defense of the faith. "Have no fear of them, nor be troubled, but in your hearts honor Christ the Lord as holy, always being prepared to make a defense to anyone who asks you for a reason for the hope that is in you" (1 Pet 3:15). Notice how Peter reminds us that in preparing a reason for the hope we have, salvation in Christ from sin, death and the devil, we "honor Christ." In no way do we supersede the work of the Holy Spirit with learning to defend the faith and then offering that evidence to unbelievers.

The resurrection is not some oddity within human history, rather it is the fulfillment of God's promise of forgiveness for those who trust in that man, Jesus Christ, whom God appointed, as Savior and Lord. Now, I have attempted to present to you the reasons or evidence for the resurrection. However, apart from understanding the moral implications of what was done on the cross, it is simply an interesting topic to be debated. I am not here to debate today; rather, I am here to present to you the fact that God has raised Jesus from the dead. Therefore, repentance is required by God.

Jesus had to be crucified, die, and be resurrected so that forgiveness in his name can be offered to all. There is no separating what occurred both physically from spiritually on the cross. Jesus died in complete fulfillment with the promises made to the prophets of old and Moses and in the Psalms.

> For those who live in Jerusalem and their rulers, because they did not recognize him nor understand the utterances of the prophets, which are read every Sabbath, fulfilled them by condemning him. And though they found in him no guilt worthy of death, they asked Pilate to have him executed. And when they had carried out all that was written of him, they took him down

---

8. Moreland, *Scaling the Secular City*, 11.

from the tree and laid him in a tomb. But God raised him from the dead. (Acts 13:27–38)

Luke's account of the resurrection emphasizes that both the death and the resurrection are grounded in the promises of God from the beginning of human history to the culmination, when the Living Christ, the Firstborn among the dead will return in power and glory.

> That very day two of them were going to a village named Emmaus, about seven miles from Jerusalem, and they were talking with each other about all these things that had happened. While they were talking and discussing together, Jesus himself drew near and went with them. But their eyes were kept from recognizing him.
>
> And he said to them, "What is this conversation that you are holding with each other as you walk?"
>
> And they stood still, looking sad. Then one of them, named Cleopas, answered him, "Are you the only visitor to Jerusalem who does not know the things that have happened there in these days?"
>
> And he said to them, "What things?"
>
> And they said to him, "Concerning Jesus of Nazareth, a man who was a prophet mighty in deed and word before God and all the people, and how our chief priests and rulers delivered him up to be condemned to death, and crucified him. But we had hoped that he was the one to redeem Israel. Yes, and besides all this, it is now the third day since these things happened. Moreover, some women of our company amazed us. They were at the tomb early in the morning, and when they did not find his body, they came back saying that they had even seen a vision of angels, who said that he was alive. Some of those who were with us went to the tomb and found it just as the women had said, but him they did not see."
>
> And he said to them, "O foolish ones, and slow of heart to believe all that the prophets have spoken! Was it not necessary that the Christ should suffer these things and enter into his glory?" And beginning with Moses and all the Prophets, he interpreted to them in all the Scriptures the things concerning himself. (Luke 24:13–25)

The subject of the historical Jesus is of great interest today. Turn on History Channel, Discovery Channel, or National Geographic and you'll see something about Jesus, his life, death, and resurrection on it. They will promote Jesus of Nazareth as a good teacher, a philosopher, a military commander, a good man even but they will not say he is God incarnate who died, was buried, and rose again according to the Scriptures as testified to by over five hundred eyewitnesses. They deny that Jesus died as a substitute for his people for the remission of their sins and that he was raised for their justification in accordance with the promises and prophecies of the Old Testament.

Those who say Jesus was a good man cannot say this without contorting their own view and the evidence in the written accounts of Jesus.

- Can a good man say he is the Messiah?
- Can a good man say he is the Son of God?
- Can a good man say he existed before Abraham was?
- Can a good man say he will rise from the dead unless he knows all these things to be true?

If in your own worldview, you think Jesus a good man but misconstrue the historical evidence in your favor, how can you cay Jesus was good? They will especially look for ways to discount the resurrection; and that's because the resurrection is not only the central focal point of our faith, it is the pivotal point upon which Christianity stands or falls, and all other doctrines are based upon this one historical fact. From this point a bridge is built to all other teachings in the Bible and clarity is given only when the resurrection is believed.

The apostle Paul wrote: "If Christ was not raised, then all our preaching is useless, and your trust in God is useless" (1 Cor 15:4) Without the resurrection, Christianity is nothing. Jesus Christ and his work of obedience, both in life and death, his perfect righteousness, his efficacious death and triumphant resurrection is what Christianity rests upon. It is Christ, and all that he encompasses, who is the cornerstone of the faith. If Jesus did not die, our sins are not paid for. If Jesus did not rise from the dead, then we have no assurance that payment made satisfaction to the Father for our sins.

Pivotal Enough to Proclaim to the World

We may still be pitied by those who do not believe the fact of the resurrection and so they will continue to think of us as very miserable people who hold on to some fairy tale or myth. However, the facts are the facts: Jesus rose bodily from the dead on the third day and ascended to heaven and sits at the right hand of the Father until he comes again to judge both the living and the dead. This my friends is what is so important. Jesus is coming again to judge everyone living and who ever lived. That is why the resurrection is pivotal to our proclamation of the gospel. If Jesus is still in the tomb, we can rightly ignore everything he said. However, if he is alive then we have a message which removes the miserable condition of the world for he is the sacrifice for the world to take away all their sins. He died so that their sins would be paid for. He lives to prove that the Father accepted his sacrifice and no longer holds our sins against us. The resurrection is what proves we are forgiven.

When speaking with your neighbor, friend, coworker, or family member, focus on the resurrection because without it we should be pitied. Yet, because he lives my sins are forgiven and theirs are too.

The resurrection is the pivotal part of proclaiming salvation to people everywhere.

> The mere regarding of the Gospel as a truthful record is not justifying faith. A person must believe it applies to him/her.
>
> —Martin Luther
>
> He ascended into heaven and sits at the right hand of God the Father Almighty. From thence He will come to judge the living and the dead.
>
> —The Apostles' Creed

So many people are curious as to when Jesus will return. In a discussion with a young boy, a neighbor, he came to me because a classmate had warned him that Jesus was coming and the world was going to be destroyed. I suppose it was her attempt at witnessing to him but all she did was make him scared. Our work of evangelism is not to scare people to Jesus but rather to tell them how he loved them so much he would die for their sins so that they might have eternal life. Here is how that event unfolded in my garden.

Strawberries, Rolly Pollies, and the Gospel

It is not every day that a visit to the doctor brings news that more blood tests must be done. Such was my day today. So, while I await the results, Lord willing next week, and trust in my Loving Heavenly Father with whatever the result, I continue to do what God has called me to do: be a good wife, serve faithfully in my vocation (professor), and love my neighbor as myself. This is where God showed me his own love for me today: in the garden with a young boy (our neighbor's son) who wanted to earn some money to buy a toy.

As we worked to weed the garden he picked clover out of the corn and onions while I picked the grass out of the strawberry patch and found some ripe strawberries that I'd missed when picking earlier in the day. He filled the bucket with weeds and I filled another with the berries. When we had finished we sat down to sort through the berries with the not-so-perfect ones being set aside as treats for the chickens. Some of these looked beautiful until we examined them and found rolly pollie (pill bug) holes in them. To my utter surprise God would use those particular strawberries to be able to explain sin to this young boy.

He began to chat with me about a girl in his class who told him that God was coming back and would destroy the world and be very angry with everyone. He said that he was scared. Earlier he had noticed my necklace which has a Lutheran Rose on it. He started to ask about it again and when I spoke of God needing to die on the cross in the center, his interest piqued even more. He asked if God made him? Was God really angry? Why did God have to die?

Enter the strawberries and rolly pollies. As we were sorting I pulled out the ones with holes and explained to him that we won't eat them since they're ruined . . . like us people. I shared creation with him and he wondered if God needed a magic wand to make everything. I shocked him by telling him that God made everything just by speaking it. His face lit up that God was more powerful and didn't need magic. Then on to Adam and how God molded him out of clay and then breathed into Adam and he was alive. Then he asked, but what happened? Nothing is perfect like you said it was. So, enter Eve and how they disobeyed God, tried to hide from him because they knew they had sinned (had to explain this to him) but how God still loved them.

Rolly-pollie-eaten strawberries were a great example of how sin destroys what was once good and that this is what sin did to us so that our hearts are "yucky" and need to be fixed. But, just like we can't fix the strawberries ourselves, because we're not God, God needed to fix our hearts so they weren't "yucky" anymore.

Enter a perfect strawberry as the example of Jesus who was perfect; he didn't kick his siblings, lie, disobey, or steal . . . ever. Wide-eyed the boy listened to every word. Explaining the cross he wondered why Jesus would have to die when he didn't do anything wrong. I shared how Jesus took all the "yuck" we do and was punished so that we wouldn't have to be and that if we believe Jesus did this that he would give us a new heart. Then I shared how Jesus didn't stay dead. To his amazement he listened to how Jesus was not a ghost but actually came back and was alive and flesh and bone just like us and how when Jesus comes back, because he promised to and since he is perfect he would never lie to us, it would be the most awesome day ever. He was amazed that God loves us so much that he would die so we wouldn't be punished for the rolly pollies in our hearts."

I have often said that God gives us opportunities to share his gospel of love and forgiveness in ways and with people and places we don't expect, so be ready for them. Never in my life did I think strawberries and rolly pollies would open the door wide for the gospel with our young neighbor.

Nunya

That's a term my darling husband, Bobby, has coined that most of our church has picked up. It simply means none of your business and it gets applied to questions about things that God has not revealed. So, what do we know about the end times? Well, for one the apostle Peter, in his first sermon (Acts 2) states that they were in the end times then. For us modern Christians, that means we've been in the end times since Pentecost. While we await the return of Christ, we should be about the Master's service in proclaiming and defending the faith.

When conversations arise about the end times we should immediately redirect the conversation back on to what we know, because quite frankly, none of us knows exactly how it will all be worked out. However, one thing we do know is that Jesus is coming again to judge the living and the dead.

That said, I try to avoid discussion about some secret rapture (that teaching began in the 1840s so should we believe that anyway) or some great tribulation or whether it's a pre-tribulation, post-tribulation, or mid-tribulation rapture. God warned us that we are not to look into the secret things that belong to him, so we should probably obey that when doing apologetics too. Besides, as Dr. Montgomery says, "Stick with what we know, as end-times information is what we know the least about."[9]

What we do want to do is continue to bring the conversation back to the facts of the faith: Jesus died, was buried, and rose again according to

9. From a private lunch in France during 2019.

the Scriptures. The church believes that at the end of the world Christ will appear for judgments raising all the dead (1 Thess 4:13—5:2). According to Matthew's Gospel Jesus will then give the godly intellect eternal life and everlasting joys while condemning the ungodly to be tormented in hell for eternity. This is a difficult subject. However we must be true to God's word when explaining that "he will come to judge the living and the dead" (2 Tim 4:1). The church does not believe there will be an end to the suffering of sinners because that is not what God's word teaches. This should be an impetus for Christians to get out there with the gospel because the world is filled with sinners in need of salvation. We may not like the idea of eternal judgment and punishment but we must believe it and also proclaim it's when asked about it. We must defend our position utilizing the Scriptures and the two easiest are the ones from Thessalonians and the Gospel of Matthew. Get those in your heart and utilize them should this topic arise. Whether they like it or not, this is to be believed so that they might have life everlasting.

Apostles' Creed Part 3

I believe in the Holy Spirit, the holy Christian Church,
the communion of saints,
the forgiveness of sins, the
resurrection of the body,
and the life everlasting. Amen.

CHAPTER 10

The "What Now?"

THE BEGINNING OF THE explanation of the third article of the Creed says

> The salvation Christ won on the cross has truly come to pass (objective reality). But unless the Holy Spirit applies that salvation to us personally and individually (subjectively), it will remain hidden from us.[1]

We come now to the section that my own pastor often refers to on the church calendar as the "what now" portion of the year. If we believe the gospel as presented in the Second Article of the Apostles' Creed how then shall we live? This section of the Creed informs us of the Holy Spirit and his work. This section, as Martin Luther says, is about "sanctification." This third article tells us of his office as Third Person of the Holy Trinity and what he does. Luther explains that the Holy Spirit makes people holy so this is the ongoing work of God in his church. Whereas the sacrificial life and death of Jesus was done in history, the Holy Spirit is continually doing his work throughout history since the fall of Adam until the return of the Lord Jesus Christ.

The Holy Spirit

What is it that the church confesses regarding the Holy Spirit? The Lutheran Church in their Augsburg Confession says that there are three persons in the Godhead the father, the son, and the Holy Spirit (Matt 28:19). This is what the Bible teaches: God the Father, God the Son and God the Holy Spirit. There are not three gods but three persons in unity of the one

---

1. Cain, "It Is Finished," para. 9.

Godhead. We do not confess heresies that arose which assumed that there are three personalities or modalities but three persons.

In the Smallcald Articles we confess that the Holy Spirit proceeds from the father and the son (John 15:26). We also hold that neither the Father nor the Holy Spirit but the Son became man. The best way to understand this is a Trinitarian formula I learned in seminary and it goes like this: the Father is God the Father, the Father is not the Son, the Father is not the Spirit. The Son is God, the Son is not the Father, the Son is not the Holy Spirit. The Holy Spirit is God, the Holy Spirit is not the Father, the Holy Spirit is not the Son. That's it. That's how to understand the triune God. As for the Holy Spirit, we confess "I believe in the Holy Spirit."

Martin Luther writes in his explanation of Article 3,

> I cannot connect this article to anything better than sanctification. Through this article the Holy Spirit, with his office, is declared and shown: he makes people holy. Therefore, we must take a stand upon the term Holy Spirit, because it is so precise and complete that we cannot find another . . . God's Spirit alone is called the Holy Spirit, that is, he who has sanctified and still sanctifies us.[2]

How does the Holy Spirit sanctify us and make us holy? He does it by the very next statements in this third article: through the holy Christian church, the communion of saints, the forgiveness of sins, the resurrection of the body, and the life everlasting. The evangelical church does not use, and many don't even know, the phrase "means of grace." So what do I mean by that term? Means of grace are the way by which God gives us the forgiveness, life, and salvation won by the death and resurrection of Christ: the gospel, absolution, baptism, and the Lord's Supper.[3]

God uses the ordinary to do the extraordinary. God uses ordinary things, what are called means, to affect His works which are extraordinary. Where we find the ordinary, water, bread, wine, and the preaching of the word of God in the hearing of our ears, is what God has chosen to use to deliver his salvation. He works through these ordinary things by the power of the Holy Spirit.

Growing up Pentecostal/Baptist we readily recognized that God had, in the past, worked through ordinary things but often denied that he still does now. We looked for "miracles" whereever we could find them. If we didn't, well, either we didn't have enough faith or perhaps our faith just

---

2. Dau, *Concordia*, 402.
3. Engelbrecht, *Lutheran Difference*, 687.

wasn't quite strong enough and that would, eventually, lead to spiritual depression or worse. You might end up wondering if God even loves you or if you are truly his.

Becoming Reformed we readily recognized that God had, in the past, worked through ordinary things but he does not do that now, unless one is thinking of God's providential works. The only ordinary things God worked through was the preaching of the word. Of course, God does work through the ordinary preaching of his word but he also works through water, bread, and wine.

So I thought I would just briefly look at what God has worked through in the past and what he works through now for the salvation of sinners.

> Ordinary bush on fire—extraordinary fire does not burn the bush (Exod 3:2)
>
> Ordinary waterway Israel must pass through—extraordinary the waters mount upwards to open a dry passageway through the waters (Exod 14:21-22)
>
> Ordinary stone—extraordinary victory over the Philistines (1 Sam 17:49)
>
> Ordinary muddy waters of Jordan—extraordinary curing of leprosy (2 Kings 5:1-14)
>
> Ordinary young virgin girl—extraordinarily becomes the mother of our Lord Jesus (Luke 1:43)
>
> Ordinary wood—extraordinary cross (John 19)
>
> Ordinary sour wine—extraordinarily fulfills prophecy (John 19:28-30)
>
> Ordinary burial tomb—extraordinary resurrection (Luke 24:1-9)

This is what God used: ordinary things (means) to bring about an extraordinary salvation (grace). These were the means of grace for God's people. Some ordinary things: stones, fire, mud, wood which God used in extraordinary ways for the good of sinners. God, however, has not stopped using the ordinary to do the extraordinary: Saving sinners from sin, death, and the devil. Here is what he still uses today:

> Ordinary water—extraordinary salvation and the forgiveness of sins (1 Peter 3:21)

THE "WHAT NOW?"

Baptism, which corresponds to this (the ark of Noah) now saves you, not as a removal of dirt from the body but as an appeal to God for a good conscience, through the resurrection of Jesus Christ.

God, working with the word in the waters of baptism actually saves you, brings forgiveness of sins, and cleanses you having washed you from all your sins. Baptism, ordinary water with the word actually buries us with Christ and raises us too in new life (regenerates us) (Rom 6:1–5). Quite an extraordinary work is done with ordinary water: Salvation from sin, death, and the devil.

> Ordinary bread—extraordinarily the true body of our Lord, given for us (Luke 22:19)
>
> Ordinary wine—extraordinarily the true blood of our Lord, given for the forgiveness of our sins (Luke 22:20)

Scripture tells us that when we partake of the bread and wine we are partaking of the true body and true blood of Christ. For it says, "The cup of blessing that we bless, is it not a participation in the blood of Christ? The bread that we break, is it not a participation in the body of Christ?" (1 Cor 10:16). Ordinary bread and wine with the word means that Christ feeds us with his true body and true blood to strengthen us in the faith for life unto godliness.

> Ordinary speaking—extraordinary power of God unto salvation

Paul tells us that the gospel is the "power of God unto salvation" (Rom 1:16) and that through the "folly of what we preach to save those who believe" (1 Cor 1:21).

Ordinary speaking and preaching the gospel, ordinary hearing through the word of God brings about an extraordinary thing: salvation from sin, death, and the devil.

God has not stopped using the ordinary to bring about the extraordinary. He continues to work through ordinary water, bread, wine, and speaking his word.

For most of my Christian life I would have only agreed with the latter; preaching of his word, to affect the salvation of sinners. However, as I read the Bible more, paying attention to what it says and not to what I had been taught or the theological hoops I'd learned to jump through, it is true, God uses these ordinary means to affect the salvation of sinners. Once forgiven in the ordinary waters of baptism with the word, he continues to use the ordinary means of grace, that the preaching of his word, the ordinary elements of bread and wine, his true body and true blood, to bring to us forgiveness, life, and salvation.

Don't despise these ordinary means for they are true gifts of God and extraordinary ways God still works within his church and at the local churches to deliver you from sin, death and the devil. Do not forsake attending the divine service and he will feed you through the ordinary means of speech, bread and wine which he turns into extraordinary means of grace in the word and his true body and true blood.

God has not stopped using ordinary people too. Don't leave the proclamation and defense of the faith to the professionals, e.g., pastors, professors and theologians. God has ordained to use the ordinary, everyday person, within their vocation as mom, dad, grandma or grandpa, farmer, fisherman, librarian, teacher, nurse, scientist, lawn mower, or gas station attendant, to bring the gospel to those who cross their paths. As a wife, author, blogger, and professor I come into contact with people you may not. However, you connect with folks I will never meet in my life. Each of us has a duty to love our neighbors by giving them the good news that Jesus paid for their sins and rose again for their justification. God used ordinary people in the Old and New Testaments and he still uses the ordinary to bring about the extraordinary.

The Holy Christian Church

Where God does this work is in the holy Christian church. There is no one who can know anything about Jesus or believe on him apart from the proclamation of the gospel. Now, you are probably talking to somebody who is not attending church and maybe never has. So the Holy Spirit works through the preaching of the word in the holy Christian church. While he is not hindered by you proclaiming the word outside of the four walls of a church building, it is in the divine service, along with Bible studies, that God uses the word of God to gift saving faith to sinners. If we don't tell others the gospel then no one will believe and this great gift of salvation would remain concealed. In order for this great gift not to remain hidden it must be proclaimed. The Holy Spirit is he who brings this gift home so that we make it our own. It is in the holy Christian church that the word is publicly proclaimed to his people. Through the preaching of both law and gospel the Holy Spirit reveals, illumines, and gifts true faith in the hearts of the hearers so that they can "understand, accept, and persevere in that word."[4]

Communion of Saints

We, Christians, are the body of Christ and his most holy church. The holy Christian church and the communion of saints could be viewed as synonymous. After all they speak of the same thing. In the Greek we call it *kyrie* and it means church. Where there is communion of saints there is the holy Christian church. The church in the common gathering of God's people here on earth. The local gathering of God's people has been referred to as the church militant. The people of God who are in heaven with him are called the church triumphant. Now granted we are still sinners at the same time saints but that is why the church means a communion of saints. It is the congregation of God. This congregation is called together by God to confess one Lord, one faith, one baptism for the forgiveness of sins. It is in this holy church and communion of saints, or congregation of saints, where forgiveness is both proclaimed and offered.

Forgiveness

As a Christian most of us were taught that we go to church, we "do church," we go to "worship." Notice the focus? Us. We. I. Church becomes something we do for God. We go to praise, sing, and drop an offering in the plate. We go and listen to the sermon, pray, and wonder if we can make it through the service for another week. Somewhere along the line, doing church became about us.

As a new Lutheran I was in for a surprise at church on Sundays. Turns out, they call it the divine service because it is where the Divine, God, serves us his people. Visit a Lutheran Sunday service and you'll be surprised to find out their hymnal is also their order of service. The pastor will tell you the page for the divine service, either Divine Service one, two, three, or four and you'll find that you are reading the service from the Lutheran Service book. It all seems a bit odd . . . err different than a modern evangelical, or even Presbyterian/reformed Christian is accustomed to. The focus is on God serving us, not us doing church.

---

4. Dau, *Concordia*, 402.

It begins with confession and absolution where together we will confess our sins and that

> We are by nature sinful and unclean. We have sinned against You in thought, word, and deed, by what we have done and by what we have left undone. We have not loved You with our whole heart; we have not loved our neighbors as ourselves. We justly deserve Your present and eternal punishment. For the sake of Your Son, Jesus Christ, have mercy on us. Forgive us, renew us, and lead us, so that we may delight in Your will and walk in Your ways to the glory of Your holy name. Amen.[5]

But then comes the part most evangelicals would be shocked at. The pastor offers absolution of our sins. We learn that "even as keys lock and unlock, so the authority to forgive and retain sins opens and closes heaven. Jesus gives two keys to His Church; One key absolves from sin and opens heaven. The other key retains sins and closes heaven to those who are impenitent.... All those who repent and ask for forgiveness of their sins are to be absolved."[6] This is also a time of the proclamation of the gospel. How does one know that they are sinner and in need of forgiveness? It has to be announced and this is done through the time of confession and absolution.

The pastor does not merely tell us that if we believe we are forgiven, rather, he proclaims to us that we are forgiven. He says, "Almighty God in His mercy has given His Son to die for you and for His sake forgives you all your sins. As a called and ordained servant of Christ, and by His authority, I therefore forgive you all your sins in the name of the Father and of the Son and of the Holy Spirit."

To wit, we all say a hearty "Amen."

From this point onward the service continues with God servicing us. He forgives us all our sins. We sing in response out of gratitude.

Fed by Christ Himself

At this point we have been forgiven, fed through the written word of God and fed by the preached word of God. All evangelical services, except the occasional Sunday, ended here. Yet, in the divine service we have one more feeding, one more act of the Divine for us. Yes, it is the Lord's Supper. "It is

---

5. Lutheran Church—Missouri Synod, *Lutheran Service Book*, 151.
6. Luther, *Luther's Small Catechism*, 315.

the true body and blood of our Lord Jesus Christ under the bread and wine, instituted by Christ Himself for us Christians to eat and to drink."[7] Here at the table "His saving death is proclaimed and the fruits of His atonement are distributed for the forgiveness of our sins."[8] God forgives us in this "great treasure" and our faith is strengthened. This "sets me free from my sinful past, in which death and the tyranny of Satan were my only future. Christ's body and blood give me a new life and a new future every day."[9]

It is in the Christian church that everything we need is offered to us. The Larger Catechism says: We shall daily receive in the Church nothing but the forgiveness of sin through the Word and signs, to comfort and encourage our consciences as long as we live here. After all, the work of Christ was that he be a propitiation for the sins of the world. It was shown when we looked at the name of Jesus it's very meaning was Savior. In Jesus Christ alone we have the forgiveness of sins. This is most certainly true and must be believed.

When neighbors ask us why we go to church we shouldn't be responding with I go to worship him. They have no clue what that means. But we need to tell them what is offered to us when we attend the divine service. We are given absolution and the forgiveness of all our sins. God gives us this forgiveness and feeds our faith so that we may serve others. When discussing the church itself, we need to focus on how God serves us in the worship service. We need to emphasize God does the work there and we receive his gifts and blessings there.

Bodily Resurrection and Eternal Life

The unbeliever and skeptic may turn the conversation on to what happens after this life. What is it that we Christians believe about eternal life or life after death? Hopefully, by this point in the conversation, we have already discussed creation and redemption which is completed in Jesus Christ, and the resurrection of Jesus. Since Jesus has been raised from the dead we, too, who believe on him, and are baptized in the waters with the word for the forgiveness of sins, shall rise with him again on that last day. When Scripture talks about a new body it is this body renewed and raised to eternal life. As Christians, we should explain to the unbeliever,

7. Luther, *Luther's Small Catechism*.
8. Luther, *Luther's Small Catechism*.
9. Luther, *Luther's Small Catechism*.

that because Jesus rose again the promise to us is that we will rise as well. The proof is in the resurrection of Jesus. We know that because he lives we will live also. This is life eternal, to believe on the Lord Jesus Christ. Life eternal will be in the presence of God the Father Almighty and Maker of heaven and earth with Jesus Christ his only Son and with the Holy Spirit, the three-in-one, Blessed Holy Trinity.

CHAPTER 11

Defending and Proclaiming the Faith

Creedal Apologetics

These articles of the Creed, therefore, divide and separate us Christians from all other people on earth. Even if all people outside Christianity—whether heathen, Turks, Jews, or false Christians and hypocrites—believe and worship only one true God, they still do not know what his mind toward them is and cannot expect any love or blessing from him. Therefore, they abide in eternal wrath and damnation. For they do not have the Lord Christ, and, besides, are not illumined and favored by any gifts of the Holy Spirit.[1]

How Did the Apostles in Acts Proclaim the Gospel?

GROWING UP IN A holiness-Pentecostal church formal study of the Scriptures was not encouraged. It was taught that since we were Spirit-baptized and have the Bible, that was all we needed to go out and tell others about Jesus. No professors or seminary training was needed. If you did feel that you needed training then two options were offered: Pentecostal Bible School or, in our denomination, live in a faith home to be trained. Still, formal education in smaller Pentecostal churches is not strongly encouraged since seminaries are the spiritual equivalent of cemeteries. In light of this I have decided, in presenting an apologetic to my Pentecostal and charismatic brothers and sister, what the apostles proclaimed as gospel in the hopes that they too will begin to put aside their own experiences and theological predilections for a truly biblical one.

1. Dau, *Concordia*, 405.

In the Acts of the Apostles there are well over fifteen sermons. Of that abundance there are ten which are Gospel presentations to both Jews, Gentile believers (converts to Judaism) and pagan Gentiles, which will enable us to see what the core message in proclaiming and defending the Christian faith. From those ten, I have selected seven to review. Learning from Peter, Stephen, and Paul will equip us with a proper apologetic/proclamation style and one that truly mirrors theirs.

The Apostles' Defense

When thinking of the church I grew up in, the charismatic fellowships I served and attended, I learned to tell others about Jesus. While the focus was more about the gifts than the Giver, nevertheless, the passion to witness was fed and only when I was a staunch Calvinist did that become less important. However, it was after my conversion to Lutheranism that the smoldering twigs that remained were fanned to become a steady burning fire. The love and passion I had to evangelize and defend the faith has burned brightly and it is the purpose for this presentation. Growing up Pentecostal, where education in theology, philosophy, and such things were not greatly encouraged, God providentially overruled that thinking and directed my steps in the direction of apologetics for my degrees. However, I have not lost sight of the fact that it is Christ we are proclaiming and the best source we have to aid us in that presentation is the Scriptures. Through lesson learned via Dr. Montgomery and Trinity Seminary, the position of logical reasoning, historical and documentary evidence was never placed above the written word of God.

Therefore, the apologetic I am offering to Christians is the pattern found in the Scriptures. It is an apostolic apologetic if there ever were one. Utilizing the sermons of the book of Acts from the evangelists, along with the Epistles from the apostles it is my desire that the reader will find the biblical pattern which indeed is the judicial and evidential apologetic that Dr. Montgomery has taught for decades. Far from placing human reasoning above the Scriptures, this pattern will give you the tools you need to defend the faith. These tools will bring you back from a subjective, personal, testimony-focused approach to that which the apostles used.

Objective Proclamation Examples

Though there are over a dozen sermons to be read in the book of Acts, seven give us a distinct patter from the Evangelists and Saint Paul, along with Stephen, to follow when engaging in apologetics. I will briefly go through them to show how they set an example for differing types of conversations with skeptics, religious people, and unbelievers.

Peter's Sermon at Pentecost: Acts 2:14–21

> But Peter, standing with the eleven, lifted up his voice and addressed them: "Men of Judea and all who dwell in Jerusalem, let this be known to you, and give ear to my words. For these people are not drunk, as you suppose, since it is only the third hour of the day. But this is what was uttered through the prophet Joel:
>
> "'And in the last days it shall be, God declares,
> that I will pour out my Spirit on all flesh,
> and your sons and your daughters shall prophesy,
> and your young men shall see visions,
>   and your old men shall dream dreams;
> even on my male servants and female servants
>   in those days I will pour out my Spirit, and they shall prophesy.
> And I will show wonders in the heavens above
>   and signs on the earth below,
>   blood, and fire, and vapor of smoke;
> the sun shall be turned to darkness
>   and the moon to blood,
>   before the day of the Lord comes, the great and magnificent day.
> And it shall come to pass that everyone who calls upon the name of the Lord shall be saved."
>
> Men of Israel, hear these words: Jesus of Nazareth, a man attested to you by God with mighty works and wonders and signs that God did through him in your midst, as you yourselves know—this Jesus, delivered up according to the definite plan and foreknowledge of God, you crucified and killed by the hands of lawless men. God

raised him up, loosing the pangs of death, because it was not possible for him to be held by it.

"Nothing is more forceful than to argue with them [skeptics] from prophecy, which was even more forceful than facts."[2] Peter, in his second letter reaffirms prophetic fulfillment and the Scriptures as a better and more reliable test than even his experiences on the Mount of Transfiguration when we writes,

> For we did not follow cleverly devised myths when we made known to you the power and coming of our Lord Jesus Christ, but we were eyewitnesses of his majesty. For when he received honor and glory from God the Father, and the voice was borne to him by the Majestic Glory, "This is my beloved Son, with whom I am well pleased," we ourselves heard this very voice born from heaven, for we were with him on the holy mountain. And we have something more sure, the prophetic word, to which you will do well to pay attention as to a lamp shining in a dark place, until the day dawns and the morning star rises in your hearts, know this first of all, that no prophecy of Scripture comes from someone's own interpretation. (2 Pet 1:16–20)

Peter is arguing from fulfilled Scripture and prophecy. As Chrysostom reiterated, nothing is more forceful than arguing from facts, eyewitness testimony, and from the Scriptures themselves in fulfilled prophecies. Further, when Christ performed miracles many rejected him. However, when Jesus quoted fulfilled prophecy the people could not dispute him. Peter is doing the same thing; arguing from the Scriptures. Peter does not base his argument on his own experiences, either on the Mount of Transfiguration or of Pentecost. Rather Peter argues from the power of God's own written word.

Immediately after quoting the fulfillment of Joel's prophecy, right before their very eyes, he moves to the gospel. Peter does not remain on what had been or was being seen and experienced but rather jumps off the testimonial point right into what was crucial to the hearers. We do well to take notice of how quickly Peter does this and copy his form moving from our own personal testimony to that which truly saves: the gospel.

In fact, Peter links what they are seeing (the fulfillment of Joel) right to the resurrection. That Jesus is risen as prophesied in Psalm 15 and now is in a position of authority as foretold in Psalm 110, Peter says that this is verified by the fact of the outpouring of the Spirit. Peter's focus

---

2. Martin, *Acts*, 28.

is no longer on the strange tongues the audience heard (which was true earthly languages) but on how that pouring out of the Holy Spirit proves the resurrection happened.

The very next thing Peter does is to remind the listeners that they crucified this Lord of Glory. With "lawless hands" they nailed the Son of God to a cross and killed him. Peter brings in the law of God when he reminds them that murdering an innocent is breaking God's commandments and they are every bit as guilty as the rulers in the Sanhedrin. Peter's use of the law is short and bitter but he does not leave them there. Peter had already given them the antidote to their sin problem when he said, "everyone who calls upon the name of the Lord shall be saved" (Acts 2:21). Peter reminds them that the resurrection of Christ was because death had no rights to him and could not hold or contain him. This is the gospel: Jesus died and rose again so that we sinners may be saved.

Peter's focus in this very first sermon of the church was not on the gifts or the tongues of fire or the experiences of the apostles and disciples gathered in the upper room on that Pentecost. Nor was his focus on the audience witnessing of this phenomena and their amazement. The focus of Peter's sermon is twofold: fulfillment of Scripture and the gospel of Christ who died and rose again for their salvation.

Too often at the church I grew up in and attended after my conversion the focus was upon the charismata, the experiences one could have through Spirit baptism. Too often the sermons preached even to the congregation were about the charismatic gifts one could have to live victoriously. The focus was on subjective experiences for today rather than the objective facts of fulfilled Scripture and the gospel. What if I did not have those experiences? Was I any less of a Christian because I lacked a "personal Pentecost"? How often I went down to the altar to repent and beg God for these subjective experiences rather than bask in the forgiveness of my sins. When the focus is upon an event that happened two thousand years ago which fulfilled Scripture in verifying the resurrection, then one ends up with a distorted gospel message to tell others. Peter reminds us in his first sermon to use the fulfillment of Scriptures and proclaim the gospel so that they may believe and be saved.

Follow the pattern set out by the apostles:

1. Testimony: The lame man walks and witnesses are astounded
2. Proclamation:

CREEDAL APOLOGETICS

    a. Christ, whom you killed

- The prophets spoke of Jesus
- They were eyewitnesses of the execution of Jesus
- Some cried out "Crucify him" when Pilate wanted to release Jesus

    b. Is risen from the dead: God raised him up from the dead.

3. Repent and be forgiven

The resurrection is proof that God is calling all people to repent of their sins and be forgiven. This is the gospel. In the same way the first evangelists and the apostles proclaimed and defended the gospel is the pattern we are to use today. Christians are to be proclaiming Christ crucified, died, and risen and not our particular theological persuasion nor our own personal experiences. Gospel proclamation must be objective because it is the only objective verifiable truth that saves.

Let us remember the pattern which Paul said was passed down (received), evidently from the first apostles:

> That Christ died for our sins in accordance with the Scripture, that he was buried, that he was raised on the third day in accordance with the Scriptures. (1 Cor 15:3–4)

Following the pattern set from the beginning at Pentecost, the apostles move from the objective truths of the death and resurrection of Jesus, verified by this miracle that could not be disputed to the call to believe and repent. The biblical gospel defense/apologetic is the death and physical resurrection of Jesus into the call to believe. The gospel call is not to remind them of a subjective experience but a verifiable miracle done in the name of Jesus and under his authority he calls men everywhere to repent. Peter consistently refers to the prophecies fulfilled in proclaiming the resurrection of Jesus.

The early church had the Scriptures, the Old Testament which testified about Jesus. This was their objective standard and must be ours as well. It is not denied that each apostle had their own personal testimony, subjective experience with the risen Christ, but that was not their focus nor motivation. What motivated them all was the resurrection of Jesus. This was the impetus behind their preaching, teaching, and defending the faith so much that most of them died a martyr's death for what they had eyewitnessed.

While they had their own subjective experience they had the Scripture which guided them in interpreting their personal experiences. Today, it seems we elevate experiences above the objective truths of the written word of God. They had to have something outside of themselves to give guidance to their subjective experience.[3]

Acts 13:16–22 (Part 1):

So Paul stood up, and motioning with his hand said:
"Men of Israel and you who fear God, listen. The God of this people Israel chose our fathers and made the people great during their stay in the land of Egypt, and with uplifted arm he led them out of it. And for about forty years he put up with them in the wilderness. And after destroying seven nations in the land of Canaan, he gave them their land as an inheritance. All this took about 450 years. And after that he gave them judges until Samuel the prophet. Then they asked for a king, and God gave them Saul the son of Kish, a man of the tribe of Benjamin, for forty years. And when he had removed him, he raised up David to be their king, of whom he testified and said, 'I have found in David the son of Jesse a man after my heart, who will do all my will.' Of this man's offspring God has brought to Israel a Savior, Jesus, as he promised."

Notice how Paul weaves his discourse from things present and from the prophets to the apostles as witnesses of the resurrection, and David bearing witness. For neither do the Old Testament proofs seem so cogent when taken by themselves, or the later testimonies apart from the former. Therefore, it is through both that he makes his discourse trustworthy.[4]

It is not surprising that Paul utilizes the same pattern for gospel proclamation and the defense of the faith. Paul, speaking to Israelites, references the prophets of old and then the gospel accounts of Jesus's life, as proof that Jesus is the Savior. Paul, at this point, focuses on the Old Testament prophecies which have been fulfilled in Jesus. Note well that Paul does not recount his experience on the road to damascus, though he will later. Rather, Paul emphasizes the prophecies of old coming to fulfillment in Jesus Christ. He points to Jesus as the Savior which was promised.

3. Christensen, "Subjective and Objective Religion."
4. Martin, *Acts*, 163.

Proclamation to the Gentiles (Unbelievers)

Thus far the sermons of the apostles to Jews and believing gentiles (those who had previously converted to Judaism) have been focused upon. However, what was the pattern when the apostles broadened their proclamation to those of the pagan world, gentiles? Do the apostles follow a pattern as described above which Peter, Stephen, and Paul used: an objective gospel? Or, does it suddenly change so that their own personal experiences and subjectivism are the focal point of their sermons, proclamation, and apologetic style.

In Acts 15 we have the issues of how the church is to deal with gentile converts. James, now a believer because of the resurrection of Jesus, references the prophets who foretold that gentiles too would believe in Jesus. Even within a church issue, who do we accept as believers and what is to be done with gentiles in the church now? James references fulfillment of prophecy.

One of the Scripture texts often used for missionary endeavors is Paul's sermon in Acts 17. In my training with Wycliffe Bible Translators, this was the go-to sermon to see how to interact with those who had never heard the gospel before in foreign lands. We were taught to follow Paul's pattern in proclaiming that Jesus saves to the unconverted. However, recalling that training we were encouraged to share with others what our personal experiences were. Sadly, the emphasis remained upon our own salvation testimony and what happened when we believed.

However, Paul does not do that with the Athenians. It is right to say that Paul sticks with the basics and "mere Christianity" for he does not talk to them of visions, dreams, personal prophecies, or the gifts he received but instead proclaims Christ and him crucified and raised from the dead.

Acts 17:19–34

And they took him and brought him to the Areopagus, saying, "May we know what this new teaching is that you are presenting? For you bring some strange things to our ears. We wish to know therefore what these things mean." Now all the Athenians and the foreigners who lived there would spend their time in nothing except telling or hearing something new.

So Paul, standing in the midst of the Areopagus, said: "Men of Athens, I perceive that in every way you are very religious. For as

I passed along and observed the objects of your worship, I found also an altar with this inscription: 'To the unknown god.' What therefore you worship as unknown, this I proclaim to you. The God who made the world and everything in it, being Lord of heaven and earth, does not live in temples made by man, nor is he served by human hands, as though he needed anything, since he himself gives to all mankind life and breath and everything. And he made from one man every nation of mankind to live on all the face of the earth, having determined allotted periods and the boundaries of their dwelling place, that they should seek God, and perhaps feel their way toward him and find him. Yet he is actually not far from each one of us, for

"'In him we live and move and have our being';
as even some of your own poets have said,
"'For we are indeed his offspring.'

Being then God's offspring, we ought not to think that the divine being is like gold or silver or stone, an image formed by the art and imagination of man. The times of ignorance God overlooked, but now he commands all people everywhere to repent, because he has fixed a day on which he will judge the world in righteousness by a man whom he has appointed; and of this he has given assurance to all by raising him from the dead."

Now when they heard of the resurrection of the dead, some mocked. But others said, "We will hear you again about this." So Paul went out from their midst. But some men joined him and believed, among whom also were Dionysius the Areopagite and a woman named Damaris and others with them.

While Paul utilizes the writings of their own poets and philosophers, he does not remain there. Reminding them that they are God's offspring, Paul immediately calls them to repentance because the man God appointed died and rose again from the dead. This is Paul's message and must be ours. Note well that the apostle did not recount his own personal experiences, his conversion testimony, his healing from blindness after encountering Jesus. Instead, Paul references the resurrection from the dead. His gospel proclamation is that Jesus died and rose again.

Paul does not proclaim an experience of some subjective opinion or feeling. Paul proclaims the One True God and Jesus Christ who is risen from the dead. Paul's style of proclamation is as follows: logical argument, then he speaks of God and who he really is, and finally repentance and salvation through the death and resurrection of Jesus Christ. "This I proclaim to you!" This we are to proclaim as well. Paul invites them "through the risen Christ, into the abundant mercy of God."[5] He does not call them into some subjective experience but into actual forgiveness of their sins through the actual and verifiable resurrection of Jesus Christ. The resurrection is objectively true and because it is verifiable, through numerous eyewitnesses, they are being offered the forgiveness of their sins.

In these passages, and there are many other sermons in Acts that have not been looked at, the pattern, used by the apostles, is clear: An objective gospel proclamation over and above a subjective presentation. What are we to learn through these passages? Again and again it has been shown that Peter, Stephen, James, and Paul all brought in the written word of God, the prophecies fulfilled, and the life and death of Jesus as his resurrection as witnessed to by their own eyes and that of several hundreds of his disciples. While testimony or miracle may be a starting point it is never the point of their message. Always the proclamation and defense of Christianity, for the apostles and others in the Bible, is the life, death, and resurrection of Jesus. That is where they begin and end.

The gospel proclamation pattern is:

- Jesus died, was buried rose again on the third day
- According to the Scriptures
- As seen by over five hundred eyewitnesses.

This is a creedal statement and one that the Apostles' Creed enjoins when we tell of Jesus who died under Pontius Pilate, was crucified, died, buried, and rose again.

As shown in the previous chapters the Apostles' Creed becomes a roadmap for us in both the defense and proclamation of the faith. Still, five words are crucial to the proclamation of the gospel which are echoed in that Creed and upon which we should say, "I believe."

---

5. Martin, *Acts*, 221.

CHAPTER 12

Carpe Diem

Five Simple Words

How can one simplify even the Apostles' Creed when defending and proclaiming the faith? Simple: By using the five words that are of the utmost importance:

>Christ died for your sins.

It is typical for conversations on the faith to last just a short few minutes and so it is critical that we Christians tell them what they need most: They are sinners in need of forgiveness and God has provided that in his Son, our Lord who died and rose again for the forgiveness of sins. Perhaps the conversation will go longer, but most of the time there is a short window of opportunity and we must seize the day (Latin *carpe diem*).

As we rely upon the Holy Spirit, whose work it is to convince, convict, and convert, we should prayerfully take every opportunity to proclaim and defend the Christian faith, the gospel of Jesus Christ, to friends, family, neighbors, coworkers, and those we interact with throughout our day. I remind us that we are to prayerfully take these opportunities because we must remember that any good defense is not a true defense unless we have submitted it to the power of God in prayer. Keep in mind, too, that God will work in his time and you may only be one link in the chain on their journey to salvation by grace through faith. Our task is to proclaim and defend and the Holy Spirit will convert. When discussing the Christian faith with unbelievers I always pray after they leave because the devil will try to snatch up that good seed you've planted. I also remember that some plant, some water, and God gives the increase. This means you may not be the first Christian to present the truths of God's word to them.

CREEDAL APOLOGETICS

What then should we be keeping in mind with a proclamation, presentation, or defense of the faith? As I said above, they are sinners in need of salvation. So, in this next section I will go into how you can bring out five words and present and defend the faith using them. May God bring about the salvation of those whom you speak with so that we, with the angels in heaven, may rejoice in one sinner who repents.

The Creed in Five Words

- The moving truck has just pulled in to the house next door.
- The new employee begins today.
- A new year at school for your children begins.

These are all new adventures that bring with them some uncertainty. Who is this new family? Is this employee going to become a friend? What type of interaction with the new teacher will happen this school year? Are they religious? Are they Christian?

In a global society such as ours they most likely will not be Christian. You now have two choices: never tell them the good news because you don't know how *or* talk to them even if you're nervous.

Most of us will be nervous when getting to know someone new. Most of us won't start the conversation about the gospel because either we think that's for pastors or we make the excuse, "I don't know what to say."

Well, first, we no longer live in a Christian society. Many of us (over fifty years old) grew up where the majority of our friends and family attended church somewhere. There was prayer in school and bibles were permitted on campus. We knew Sundays the neighbors were most likely at church in the morning.

Today it is completely different. As my husband and I pull out of our driveway early Sunday morning, everyone else's car/truck is still parked and the lights are usually out in their homes. As we drive through town, where there usually isn't too much traffic, on Sundays there is almost no traffic except those going to the Mormon Stake House. We arrive at church having been the lone car on the drive, for the most part.

Secular World

We live in a secular world. Sadly, even for Christians, church is not important. Of course that is probably because church has become so law driven (you must obey the command to come, you must do something for God) that people figure they can worship God in their own way and not be bound up with duty. Scripture, though, gives a completely different reason for going: God wants to serve you through the forgiveness of your sins and strengthening your faith through the preached word and the Lord's Supper.

So, your neighbor no longer attends church, maybe they never did. Their children have no idea of the reason behind Christmas and Easter and schools no longer call those days off after the holiday but instead Winter and Spring Breaks. The gospel is removed from their life and in our society they probably have never even heard it. What are you to do? You're a mom, dad, wife, husband, aunt, uncle, and not a pastor. You never went to Bible school. You're not a seminary graduate. You've never studied other religions or the Bible formally. What can you say?

Five simple words. Five words that can change their life here and eternally. Five. That seems easy enough. Count the fingers on your hand; one, two, three, four, five. That's it. What are these words? Are they easy to remember? If you're a believer you know them already:

Christ died for your sins.

That's it? That's all you need to learn? In essence, Yes. Let me break it down.

First Corinthians 15 says,

> For I delivered to you as of first importance what I also received:
> that Christ died for our sins in accordance with the Scriptures.

Hey, that's a lot more than five words. Nope. Take a closer look. Here, let me highlight them for you:

> For I delivered to you as of first importance what I also received:
> that *Christ died for our sins* in accordance with the Scriptures.

Paul is sharing about the Lord's Supper and the simple creed that he was taught about it, about the life, death and resurrection of Jesus Christ. Here within that statement are the five words you need to know to tell others about Jesus: Christ died for our sins.

Now, let me break it down for you so that you can share with the unchurched around you or the neighbor/friend/teacher/coworker/etc. that might even be of a different religion. (Also, many of your evangelical friends suffer from the pendulum swing of pride and despair because they have a debilitated gospel, so it's good for them too.)

Christ.

What do we mean? Who are we talking about? Okay, for all you non-theologians without formal Bible training you know who this is: Jesus. Christ means "anointed one." So, Jesus was set apart by God to die for our sins. As we looked at what we confess in the Apostles' Creed it is that Jesus is the Christ with all that it entails.

Died.

Yes, this Jesus died. He was crucified (you all know Passion Week and Good Friday) by the Roman leader after the Jewish religious leaders had him arrested. He did nothing wrong (sin) his entire life and only raised others from the dead, healed them, and taught them about God. This Jesus did really and actually die. In this book we looked at the crucifixion of Jesus in all its brutality. We learned that he did actually die and then was buried. It's the "why" that must be emphasized: for the forgiveness of all our sins. Then we learned that after his death was confirmed, they buried him.

Don't leave Jesus in the tomb here because he isn't there. All other leaders and founders of religions still remain in their tomb. They're dead. Jesus is alive.

This is the pivot point in your conversation. You've told them about Jesus. You told them he died. Well, we all die. What makes his death any different? This next word is what the next two hinges upon.

For.

Why? If Jesus was chosen and set apart by God, why did he have to die? If he did nothing wrong, why was he tortured on a cross? What does it matter to me? We all die.

Our.

That's everybody. That's not just some people but every single person ever conceived in this world. You. Me. Neighbor. Teacher. Store clerk. Employee. Employer. Every single person who ever lived and died is included in this word. Ours. Yours. Mine. Everyone. That means this message is for the unchurched, the irreligious, the religious or spiritual, even the evangelical who doubts their salvation. This includes . . . well, *everybody*.

Sins.

Oh . . . hold on there. Wait just one minute. Sins? Are you telling me I'm not good enough? Are you getting all religious on me now? Well, quite frankly, yes. See, we have all sinned. (Oh, that's in the Bible too in Romans 3:23: For we have all sinned and fallen short of the glory of God.)

This is where you can share that you too don't even measure up to your own standards. Talk to them about how you're not a great parent, you lose your cool with your children or others. Be honest. You too are a great sinner in need of a greater Savior (Jesus Christ). This is where they'll balk at your message (the gospel) but this is what they need to hear so desperately. Tell them that this is exactly what Jesus died for (remember that pivotal point?). Explain to them that this is exactly why Jesus is the one chosen for this task. Teach them that this is the reason he died and rose again for everyone. Proclaim the gospel to them.

If you just shared these five words with them . . . guess what, you just defended and proclaimed the gospel of Jesus Christ. You just shared that salvation has come to them that day so do not reject it but believe and be baptized for the forgiveness of their sins.

We live in a world where your neighbor, coworker/employee, friends, family, your child's teacher, or others within your social circle will no longer go to church unless they are already believers in Jesus Christ. Sadly, many believers also reject the divine service because it becomes a chore and something they have to do, aka law and not gospel. So, it is up to the people in the pew to proclaim this fantastic, amazing, awesome good news, the gospel of Jesus Christ, to them through our conversations.

I know it is hard. I may seem to be bold and outspoken, and to many I am, but I still get nervous. My heart flutters, the elephants trample in my stomach, my knees knock, and my hands gets all sweaty, but when you realize that the fires of hell are licking at their heels and they will not "hear without someone preaching/proclaiming" (Rom 10:14) then it will need to be you who have beautiful feet to proclaim the good news. Since faith comes by hearing and hearing through the word of Christ, I encourage you to throw caution to the wind and proclaim Christ died for *your* sins to your neighbor (and remember, Jesus taught the world is our neighbor in Luke 10:25–37).

Five words. Five very important words. Five life-giving and life-altering, well, okay, eternity-altering words. Just five.

As you use the Apostles' Creed to guide you in both the defense and proclamation of the faith, it may be used by God's Holy Spirit to grow your own faith as you declare with the ancient church and contemporary one when you confess:

> I believe in God, the father Almighty, maker of heaven and earth.
> And in Jesus Christ, his only son, our Lord, who was conceived by the Holy Spirit, born of the Virgin Mary, suffered under Pontius Pilate, was crucified, died and was buried. He descended into hell. The third day he rose again from the dead. He ascended into heaven and sits at the right hand of God the Father Almighty. From thence he will come to judge the living and the dead
> I believe in the Holy Spirit, the holy Christian Church, the communion of saints, the forgiveness of sins, the resurrection of the body, and the life everlasting. Amen.

Let this be enough about the Creed to lay a foundation.

—Martin Luther, Large Catechism

Appendix

Old Roman Symbol (Creed)

I believe in God the Father almighty;

and in Christ Jesus His only Son, our Lord,

Who was born of the Holy Spirit and the Virgin Mary,

Who under Pontius Pilate was crucified and buried,

on the third day rose again from the dead,

ascended to heaven,

sits at the right hand of the Father,

whence He will come to judge the living and the dead;

and in the Holy Spirit,

the holy Church,

the remission of sins,

the resurrection of the flesh

(the life everlasting).

Apostles' Creed

I believe in God, the Father Almighty, maker of heaven and earth. And in Jesus Christ, His only Son, our Lord, who was conceived by the Holy Spirit, born of the Virgin Mary, suffered under Pontius Pilate, was crucified, died and was buried.

He descended into hell. The third day He rose again from the dead. He ascended into heaven and sits at the right hand of God the Father Almighty. From thence He will come to judge the living and the dead.

I believe in the Holy Spirit, the holy Christian Church, the communion of saints, the forgiveness of sins, the resurrection of the body, and the life everlasting. Amen.

The Interrogatory Creed of Hippolytus (approximately 215 AD)

"Do you believe in God, the Father Almighty?"

"Do you believe in Christ Jesus, the Son of God, who was born of the Virgin Mary, and was crucified under Pontius Pilate, and was dead and buried, and rose again the third day, alive from the dead, and ascended into heaven, and sat at the right hand of the Father, and will come to judge the living and the dead?"

"Do you believe in the Holy Spirit, in the holy church, and the resurrection of the body?"

The Baptismal Creed of Jerusalem: The Mystagogy

(Known from fourth century patriarch Cyril of Jerusalem's Catechetical Lectures)

I believe in one God, the Father Almighty, Maker of heaven and earth, and of all things visible and invisible;

And in one Lord Jesus Christ, the only begotten Son of God, begotten of the Father before the ages, true God, by whom all things were made, who was incarnate and made man, crucified and buried, and rose again on the third day, and ascended into the heavens, and sat down at the right hand of the Father, and is coming to judge quick and dead.

And in the Holy Ghost, the Paraclete, who spake by the prophets;

And in one holy catholic Church; and resurrection of the flesh; and in life everlasting.

APPENDIX

Athanasian Creed

Whosoever will be saved, before all things it is necessary that he hold the Catholic Faith. Which Faith except everyone do keep whole and undefiled, without doubt he shall perish everlastingly. And the Catholic Faith is this: That we worship one God in Trinity, and Trinity in Unity, neither confounding the Persons, nor dividing the Substance. For there is one Person of the Father, another of the Son, and another of the Holy Ghost. But the Godhead of the Father, of the Son, and of the Holy Ghost, is all one, the Glory equal, the Majesty co-eternal. Such as the Father is, such is the Son, and such is the Holy Ghost. The Father uncreated, the Son uncreated, and the Holy Ghost uncreated. The Father incomprehensible, the Son incomprehensible, and the Holy Ghost incomprehensible. The Father eternal, the Son eternal, and the Holy Ghost eternal. And yet they are not three eternals, but one eternal. As also there are not three incomprehensibles, nor three uncreated, but one uncreated, and one incomprehensible. So likewise the Father is Almighty, the Son Almighty, and the Holy Ghost Almighty. And yet they are not three Almighties, but one Almighty. So the Father is God, the Son is God, and the Holy Ghost is God. And yet they are not three Gods, but one God. So likewise the Father is Lord, the Son Lord, and the Holy Ghost Lord. And yet not three Lords, but one Lord. For like as we are compelled by the Christian verity to acknowledge every Person by himself to be both God and Lord, So are we forbidden by the Catholic Religion to say, There be three Gods, or three Lords. The Father is made of none, neither created, nor begotten. The Son is of the Father alone, not made, nor created, but begotten. The Holy Ghost is of the Father and of the Son, neither made, nor created, nor begotten, but proceeding. So there is one Father, not three Fathers; one Son, not three Sons; one Holy Ghost, not three Holy Ghosts. And in this Trinity none is afore, or after other; none is greater, or less than another; But the whole three Persons are co-eternal together and co-equal. So that in all things, as is aforesaid, the Unity in Trinity and the Trinity in Unity is to be worshipped. He therefore that will be saved must think thus of the Trinity. Furthermore, it is necessary to everlasting salvation that he also believe rightly the Incarnation of our Lord Jesus Christ. For the right Faith is, that we believe and confess, that our Lord Jesus Christ, the Son of God, is God and Man; God, of the substance of the Father, begotten before the worlds; and Man of the substance of his Mother, born in the world; Perfect God and perfect Man, of a reasonable soul and human flesh subsisting. Equal to the Father, as touching his Godhead; and inferior to the Father, as

APPENDIX

touching his manhood; Who, although he be God and Man, yet he is not two, but one Christ; One, not by conversion of the Godhead into flesh but by taking of the Manhood into God; One altogether; not by confusion of Substance, but by unity of Person. For as the reasonable soul and flesh is one man, so God and Man is one Christ; Who suffered for our salvation, descended into hell, rose again the third day from the dead. He ascended into heaven, he sitteth at the right hand of the Father, God Almighty, from whence he will come to judge the quick and the dead. At whose coming all men will rise again with their bodies and shall give account for their own works. And they that have done good shall go into life everlasting; and they that have done evil into everlasting fire. This is the Catholic Faith, which except a man believe faithfully, he cannot be saved.

Mayo Clinic Study on Roman Crucifixion

https://tinyurl.com/y5e6jyfc

On my blog, Lutherangirl, you will find a landing page to all resources and various Christian Creeds for this book:

https://www.lutherangirl.org/post/creeds-of-old

Sing the Faith: Luther's Smaller Catechism put to music available at cph.org here

https://tinyurl.com/y4ytpzm5

We All Believe in One True God:

https://hymnary.org/text/we_all_believe_in_one_true_god_who_creat

Bibliography

Almodovar, Nancy. *A Modern Ninety-Five: Questions Today's Evangelicals Need to Answer.* Eugene, OR: Resource, 2008.
Althaus, Paul. *The Theology of Martin Luther.* Philadelphia: Fortress, 1966.
Anderson, Norman. *Christianity and Comparative Religion.* Downers Grove, IL: InterVarsity, 1971.
———. *Christianity and World Religions: The Challenge of Pluralism.* Downers Grove, IL: InterVarsity, 1984.
"Apostolic Constitutions." https://www.newadvent.org/fathers/0715.htm.
Atchley, Rachel M., and Mary L. Hare. "Memory for Poetry: More Than Meaning?" *International Journal of Cognitive Linguistics* 4.1 (2013) 35–50. https://www.ncbi.nlm.nih.gov/pmc/articles/PMC4577018/.
Barth, Karl. *Dogmatics in Outline.* New York: Harper Torchbooks, 1959.
Bruce, F. F. *The Books and the Parchments: How We Got Our English Bible.* Rev. ed. Old Tappan, NJ: Revell, 1984.
Christensen, Otto H. "Subjective and Objective Religion (Part 1)." *Ministry International Journal for Pastors,* November 1965. https://www.ministrymagazine.org/archive/1965/11/subjective-and-objective-religion.
Costello, A. V. "Early Christian Creeds and Their Importance for Apologetics: Part II—The Nicene Creed." *Theological Apologetics* (blog), December 15, 2018. http://theologicalapologetics.com/2018/12/15/the-early-creeds-and-their-importance-for-apologetics-part-ii-the-nicene-creed/.
Cox, Harvey. *Fire from Heaven: The Rise of Pentecostal Spirituality and the Reshaping of Religion in the Twenty-first Century.* Reading, MA: Addison-Wesley, 1995.
Craig, William Lane. *The Kalām Cosmological Argument.* London: Palgrave Macmillan, 1979.
"Crucifixion." https://web.archive.org/web/20120203172147/http://www.frugalsites.net/jesus/crucifixion.htm.
Dau, William Hermann Theodore. *Concordia: the Lutheran Confessions: A Reader's Edition of the Book of Concord.* 2nd ed. St. Louis, MO: Concordia, 2005.
Edwards, William D., et al. "On the Physical Death of Jesus Christ." *The Journal of the American Medical Association* 255.11 (1986) 1455–63.
Engelbrecht, Edward A., ed. *The Lutheran Difference: An Explanation & Comparison of Christian Beliefs.* St. Louis, MO: Concordia, 2010.

BIBLIOGRAPHY

Engelbrecht, Edward A., et al., eds. "Philippians 2:9-11." In *The Lutheran Study Bible: English Standard Version*, 2035. Saint Louis: Concordia, 2009.

Fabien, Créteur. "Evangelism as a Testimony." *Sermon Central*, December 2, 2003. https://www.sermoncentral.com/sermons/evangelism-as-a-testimony-creteur-fabien-sermon-on-evangelism-how-to-63825?ref=AllSermonPrep.

González, Justo L. *The Apostles' Creed for Today*. Louisville: Westminster John Knox, 2007.

Greenleaf, Simon. "Testimony of the Evangelists by Simon Greenleaf (1783–1853)." http://law2.umkc.edu/faculty/projects/ftrials/jesus/greenleaf.html.

Habermas, Gary. "The Minimal Facts Approach to the Resurrection of Jesus: The Role of Methodology as a Crucial Component in Establishing Historicity." *Southern Theological Review* 3.1 (Summer 2012) 15–26.

Hyde, Daniel. "Creeds and Confessions: Biblical and Beneficial." *Ligonier Ministries* (blog), September 5, 2014. https://www.ligonier.org/blog/creeds-confessions-biblical-beneficial/.

Irenaeus, Saint. "Chapter 10: The Rule of the Truth Is One in the Church throughout the World." In *St. Irenaeus of Lyons: Against the Heresies, Volume 1, Book 1*, edited by Walter J. Burghardt and translated by Dominic J. Unger, 48–50. Ancient Christian Writers 55. New York: Newman, 2010.

Jacobsen, Douglas. *Thinking in the Spirit: Theologies of the Early Pentecostal Movement*. Bloomington, IN: Indiana University Press, 2003.

Kelly, J. N. D. *Early Christian Creeds*. 3rd ed. New York: Continuum, 2006.

Kenyon, Frederic. *The Bible and Archaeology*. New York: Harper, 1940.

Klemm, William R. "Does Music Help Memory?" *Psychology Today*, December 1, 2013. https://www.psychologytoday.com/us/blog/memory-medic/201312/does-music-help-memory.

Leach, Charles, and R. A. Torrey. *Our Bible: How We Got It and Ten Reasons Why I Believe the Bible Is the Word of God*. Chicago: Revell, 1898.

Lewis, C. S. *Mere Christianity*. New York: Harper One, 2001.

Luther, Martin. *Luther's Small Catechism with Explanation*. Saint Louis: Concordia, 2017.

Lutheran Church—Missouri Synod. *Lutheran Service Book: Three-year Lectionary*. St. Louis, MO: Concordia, 2006.

Martin, Francis, ed. *Acts*. Vol. 5 of *Ancient Christian Commentary on Scripture, New Testament*. Downers Grove, IL: InterVarsity, 2006.

Montgomery, John Warwick. *Defending the Biblical Gospel*. Alberta, CA: Canadian Institute for Law, Theology and Public Policy, 1997.

———. *Faith Founded on Fact: Essays in Evidential Apologetics*. Nashville, TN: Nelson, 1978.

Moreland, J. P. *Kingdom Triangle: Recover the Christian Mind, Renovate the Soul, Restore the Spirit's Power*. Grand Rapids, MI: Zondervan, 2009.

———. *Scaling the Secular City: A Defense of Christianity*. Grand Rapids, MI: Baker, 1987.

Netland, Harold. *Evangelical Apologetics*. Camp Hill, PA: Christian Publications, 1996.

Paul, Annie Murphy. "How Music Can Improve Memory." https://www.kqed.org/mindshift/31512/how-music-can-improve-memory.

Peters, Albrecht. "Luther's Understanding of the Apostles' Creed within the Context of the Creedal-Tradition of Western Christendom." In *Commentary on Luther's Catechisms*, translated by Thomas H. Trapp, 3–56. Creed ed. Saint Louis, MO: Concordia, 2011.

Pliny the Younger. "Pliny the Younger and Trajan on the Christians." http://www.earlychristianwritings.com/text/pliny.html.

BIBLIOGRAPHY

Roberts, Alexander, and James Donaldson, eds. *The Apostolic Fathers*. Vol. 1, *Ante-Nicene Christian Library*. Norderstedt, Germany: Hansebooks GmbH, 2016. https://www.ccel.org/ccel/schaff/anf01.i.html.

Rubin, D. C. *Memory in Oral Traditions: The Cognitive Psychology of Epic, Ballands, and Counting-out Rhymes*. New York: Oxford University Press, 1995.

Schaff, Philip. "Confessiones Ecclesiae Apostolicae: Scripture Confessions." In *The Creeds of Christendom*, 2:3–92. 3 vols. 1983. Reprint, Grand Rapids, MI: Baker, 1996.

———. "Name and Definition." In *The Creeds of Christendom*, edited by Philip Schaff, 1:4. 3 vols. 1983. Reprint, Grand Rapids, MI: Baker, 1996.

Schaff, Philip, ed. *A Select Library of the Nicene and Post-Nicene Fathers of the Christian Church*. First Series. 14 vols. Grand Rapids, MI: Eerdmans, 1956.

Sire, James W. *A Little Primer on Humble Apologetics*. Downers Grove, IL: InterVarsity, 2006.

Sproul, R. C., ed. *The Reformation Study Bible: English Standard Version*. Phillipsburg, NJ: Presbyterian and Reformed, 2005.

Wengert, Timothy J., ed. *Dictionary of Luther and the Lutheran Traditions*. Grand Rapids, MI: Baker Academic, 2017.

Wimber, John. *Kingdom Evangelism: Proclaiming the Gospel in Power*. Ann Arbor, MI: Vine, 1989.

Wolfmueller, Bryan. *Has American Christianity Failed?* St. Louis, MO: Concordia, 2016.

www.ingramcontent.com/pod-product-compliance
Lightning Source LLC
Chambersburg PA
CBHW072136160426
43197CB00012B/2124